Express Lanes & Country Roads

The Way We Lived in North Carolina, 1920–1970

© 1983 The University of North
Carolina Press

Manufactured in the United States
of America

*Library of Congress Cataloging in
Publication Data*
Parramore, Thomas C.
   Express lanes & country roads.

   Bibliography: p.
   1. North Carolina—Economic
conditions. 2. North Carolina—Social
conditions. I. Nathans, Sydney.
II. North Carolina. Dept. of Cultural
Resources. III. Title. IV. Title:
Express lanes and country roads.
HC107.N8P37 1983   975.6′042
      82-21747
ISBN 0-8078-1553-5
ISBN 0-8078-4105-6 (pbk.)

Express Lanes & Country Roads

The Way We Lived in North Carolina, 1920–1970

Published for the North Carolina Department of Cultural Resources

by The University of North Carolina Press   *Chapel Hill*

Editor:
Sydney Nathans

Consultants:
Thomas H. Clayton
Larry Misenheimer
William S. Price, Jr.

This publication has been made possible through a grant from the National Endowment for the Humanities.

The Way We Lived series was developed under the guidance of the Historic Sites Section, Division of Archives and History, North Carolina Department of Cultural Resources.

(Title page) N.C. State Archives. Cafeterias were a new development in this era. This photograph, like many others in this book, is part of the Barden Collection of pictures taken by Albert Barden and his father, commercial photographers. The Barden family came from England in 1907 and for almost the next fifty years recorded life in Raleigh.

(Opposite) Hillsboro Street, Raleigh, at North Carolina State College entrance, 1921. N.C. State Archives.

Christine Alexander took the photographs not otherwise credited in this book.

Text by Thomas C. Parramore

Research and Marginalia by Jean B. Anderson

Design and Art Editing by Christine Alexander

Experiencing History

This series of books, *The Way We Lived*, is based on the premise that the past can be most fully comprehended through the combined impact of two experiences: reading history and visiting historic places. The text of this volume (the fifth in a series of five) is therefore coordinated with a variety of historical sites. Most places pictured as well as those mentioned in the margins are open to the public regularly or by appointment. Information about visiting and exact locations may be obtained locally.

The closer we are to history the harder it is to perceive. This book describes the main events and movements of the immediate past that affected everyday life and points out places to look for evidence of that past. It tries to make the reader sensitive to the local scene and to recognize in a factory, highway, or park its real meaning. Whether connected with an important action, a disappearing custom, or a far-reaching concept, the sites mentioned in this volume (and they are only a handful of what the reader can find) make plain and palpable the way North Carolinians lived in the most recent past.

Contents

Village general store, Wendell, Wake County, ca. 1938. Howard W. Odum Subregional Photo Study.

Lucy Spencer of Stokes County remembered how she "used to go down to the store every night. That was a regular hangout for everybody in this neighborhood. Didn't matter how dark, how cold the weather was, we'd all try to get down there. Just an old country store. Sold everything from pickles to shoes. Pretty good line of shoes, too. 'Course we didn't go to buy anything 'specially. We just went." Ginns, *Rough Weather Makes Good Timber.*

Overview

Although the frontier disappeared in North Carolina before the Revolutionary War, the frontier spirit lived on in the Tar Heel state well into the twentieth century. The ingredients of that spirit included a hardy frontier individualism that made each man the master of his own fortunes and the cause of his own shortcomings. In early times, this spirit had its most striking form in the *code duello* of the well-to-do and the gouging match of the common citizen. In recent times, it has manifested itself in a marked suspicion of any scheme designed to cast people together in organizational patterns or cooperative enterprises. Early and late, it has included a tendency to view government at all levels as a potential menace to the freedom and pocketbooks of individual citizens.

The period covered by this volume witnessed a considerable erosion of this spirit, though not its disappearance. Along with certain traits of the frontier character—exclusive concern for one's own locality, mistrust of the alien in idea as well as in person—rugged individualism accounts for other of the distinguishing features of native Tar Heel thought and behavior. In time past, it meant that North Carolina was the next to last state to adopt the federal Constitution and the last to join the Confederacy. In the twentieth century, it has meant the repeated rejection of the Equal Rights Amendment and a general skepticism toward national initiatives in the realms of civil rights and social reforms.

Between 1920 and 1970 North Carolina's frontier spirit was assailed by powerful forces from elsewhere in the nation and beyond its borders. North Carolinians remained throughout this half-century generally leery of "isms," of panaceas, of mere good intentions, of moral calls-to-arms. But Tar Heels still managed to find within themselves the flexibility to avoid outright confrontation with what appeared to be the undeniable will of the American people.

From a distance, the fact that a handful of articulate liberal spokesmen were tolerated and even admired in North Carolina helped give the state a reputation for progressivism beyond its neighbors. Other Americans were likely to identify North Carolina with the ideas of prominent sons such as playwright Paul Green, university president Frank Porter Graham, or editors Gerald W. Johnson and Josephus Daniels. Within the state, the views of such people were as likely to be suspect.

By the end of World War II, North Carolinians were startled to find themselves the beneficiaries of a good deal of praise and publicity from other quarters. Political analyst V. O. Key in 1949 described "progressive plutocracy" as the prevailing strength of the state in the first half of the century. In his view, a comfortable understanding between business and government leaders worked to the advantage of the state and its citizens. In comparison with other southern states, Key found North Carolinians more "energetic and ambitious" and possessing "a closer approximation to national norms, or national expectations of performance." No major scandals tainted the seats of state power, no demagogues disgraced its public deliberations. The state's economy was "virile and balanced"; its people enjoyed a reputation "for fair dealings with its Negro citizens. . . . nowhere has cooperation between white and Negro leadership been more effective."

Even historian Arnold J. Toynbee found reasons to celebrate North Carolina's more impressive national image in the twentieth century than those of Virginia or South Carolina, which historians had once favored. Toynbee adopted Key's explanation that North Carolina, having less to lose in the way of plantations, slaves, and grandeur, had suffered less profoundly from the Civil War than her neighbors. He claimed to find "up-to-date industries, mushroom universities and a breath of the hustling, 'boosting' spirit which [one] has learnt to associate with the 'Yankees' of the North." *National Geographic* magazine gave the image the stamp of official endorsement in 1962. In an article entitled "Dixie Dynamo," it represented North

Horse-drawn road grader, ca. 1920s. N.C. State Archives.

2

Carolina as having "something inspiring" about it, "something exciting, dynamic, and somehow youthful." North Carolina, it seemed, had finally arrived.

Perhaps all this was a bit too much. Though the cause of social justice moved forward in North Carolina, organized labor made little headway in these years. Industrial gains were impressive; nonetheless, per capita income remained tragically low. A code of civility cushioned relations between the races, but it also made the rising challenge to segregation seem a matter of bad manners. Still, the enthusiasm of outsiders was not misplaced. As in much of the rest of the nation, the average citizen's standard of living expanded to embrace the automobile, electric utilities, and a busy regimen of recreation and cultural enlightenment.

The half-century ending in 1970 saw the construction here of the nation's longest state-maintained system of roads, the establishment of great national forests and state parks, the emergence of a vast panoply of tourist accommodations. It was an age that saw the beginnings of a vital movement in historic preservation from the Outer Banks to the Great Smoky Mountains. Education and health care, literature and art, were far superior at the end of the period to what they had been at the outset.

From as little distance as a decade later, Tar Heels could look back on the half-century with no little satisfaction at what they had accomplished and with greater confidence in their ability to resolve other problems. In terms of their willingness and capacity to respond to challenges, Tar Heels found that they had lost none of their old frontier spirit. They anticipated that the next half-century would be still better than the last.

The urge of growing numbers of Tar Heels to identify themselves with, and participate more fully in, the national experience mirrored the resurgence of American strength and prosperity. For the nation, the sobering disillusions of a decade of economic malaise after 1929 were all but forgotten in the 1940s. Never had the virtues of capitalism and democracy appeared more unassailable, whatever the momentary success of the Soviet Union might mean.

It was not just material abundance and vindicated democracy that the nation claimed for itself but a higher moral vision: a vision of a world without racial antagonisms, religious discord, or ethnocentric squabbles. The employment of the states' rights doctrine as a shield against that vision made the doctrine's proponents seem mean-spirited and vicious. Never had the ethical ideals of the nation as a whole seemed more demonstrably just and high-minded. The nation that defeated fascism undertook the construction of a more humane social order abroad and at home.

Perhaps the Red Scare of the 1920s and the McCarthy Purges of the 1950s should have suggested more forcefully than they did an element of delusion in the nation's ambitious image of itself. But the shock waves of the 1960s went far toward weakening faith, at home and abroad, in the permanence and benevolence of the national creed. By 1970 the assassinations of prominent leaders, the aroused protests of minorities, and the quagmire of foreign war had brought Americans to a period of uncommon introspection and self-examination.

No longer was it quite so certain that the world only hungered to share our vision, to be guided by our inspiration and secured by our might. It had taken the experience of half a century to drive home this lesson, to cast the shadow of realism over the glittering vista of idealism. Perhaps in the long run the nation would be better for it, but the immediate effect was a reassessment of the headlong drive of various states and sections to make a seat for themselves on the national bandwagon. Already by 1970 one heard talk of a "New Federalism" that emphasized self-help and localism in attacking social and other problems.

4

North Carolinians drew different conclusions from two decades of change and turmoil. For some, the lesson was that society should abandon altogether collective efforts to remake itself in any image and leave it to individuals once more to strive as best they could for themselves. For others, the state seemed infinitely richer in spirit and talent as a consequence of the barriers broken and programs created through social struggle. Perhaps all North Carolinians might begin to look to their own peculiar heritage for guidance and inspiration. For there were values in that heritage that had nothing to do with oppression of the weak or exploitation of the underprivileged. States' rights and localism did not necessarily mean the reign of bigotry but could as readily mean a fuller participation of the individual in the life of the community, a closer bond between leaders and led. Or so it appeared as the state and nation came to assess a second century of their experience and to prepare for the challenges of a third.

5

The Sod-Busters

"Hog and Hominy" Days

Between 1920 and 1950, for better or worse, the life of the farmer was transformed. Once crowded, the country seemed empty. "The people are gone!" reported those who remained. Machinery replaced mules and men. Tenants and sharecroppers, once a majority of those who tilled the soil, had virtually disappeared. Less visibly, giant corporations and government agencies gradually replaced many family farms. Agriculture had become a large-scale business.

A social historian of the 1930s claimed for the typical North Carolinian five characteristic attitudes: conservatism, individualism, provincialism, sectionalism, and superstition. In these traits Tar Heels of the early twentieth century preserved their continuity and identity with the pioneers of the eighteenth century. And, though none of these attitudes disappeared between 1920 and 1970, none escaped the assault of the new forces that stirred the hemisphere and swept the nation.

Among the eddies and currents that affected farmers in North Carolina, the most obvious to many Americans were those that exerted themselves from the outside. The coming of the tractor in the 1920s and 1930s, the widespread introduction of electric power in the 1940s and 1950s, the growth of schools and transport facilities, and the vigorous economic interventionism of the New Deal were among the most significant of these. Slowly, often reluctantly, farmers bowed to the necessity of becoming agricultural technicians, mechanics, electricians. They acknowledged the need to surrender a measure of their independence to the dictates of distant bureaucrats. But they were equally aware of internal changes in the way farmers related to one another and to the nonfarming society. These included novel forms of cooperative enterprise, new arrangements for ownership, and new marketing techniques. Inevitably, such agents of change sooner or later profoundly affected family relationships and transformed the quality of daily living—not always in agreeable ways.

Only Texas had more farms than North Carolina in 1920. Across the nation the number of farms had peaked, but this would not happen in North Carolina for another thirty years. Cotton, artificially spurred on by wartime and postwar demand, briefly overtook tobacco as the state's leading cash crop. Corn, sweet potatoes, peanuts, and soybeans were other major crops, placing North Carolina among the top seven states in the annual value of farm produce.

"Farmers say a good fence should be horse high, bull strong, and pig tight." Cox, *Southern Sidelights*.

7

Late Snow at Riverwood. Courtesy Bob Timberlake.

Mollie Alderman of Duplin County remembered the depression: "In Hoover time my sister-in law's husband gave us a squirrel an' we cooked that squirrel three times. The first time we cooked it we put dumplins in 'im. Next meal comes along we put pastry on 'im, an' the next time we put rice in there. An' that was the last of that squirrel. That Hoover almost perished us to death." Wolcott, *Rose Hill.*

Half a century later, nostalgia had transformed the hardships and deprivation of the depressed interwar years into "hog and hominy days," when the sturdy yeomen lived contentedly on the simple abundance of nature. *Of Mules and Memories* is a wistful backward glance by a Tar Heel writer of the 1970s; *Rough Weather Makes Good Timber: Carolinians Recall* is another. Artist Bob Timberlake won acclaim largely by painting scenes that evoked the cherished images of more rural times and places.

Old-timers in an urban and industrial age remember with special fondness the farm barns of their adolescence, the big cornfields, the vast cribs where the corn was stored, and aromatic smokehouses in which corn-fed pork was cured. During the depression years, as in earlier times, cattle and hogs foraged for themselves in woods and fields and returned in the evening to the high-pitched summons of the cattle call and "coor pig" that resounded across bucolic distances. In the fall, hogs were penned and fattened on "slops" from the kitchen, sweet potatoes, and such corn as was unfit for either people or cattle.

Hog-killing, like corn-shucking or wood-cutting time, was a social occasion during which neighbors gathered to divide the hundred separate chores that had to be performed. Hog killing began soon after the first heavy frosts in December or January, the men going down to the pens in early morning to shoot and bleed the selected hogs. The carcasses were dumped into a vat of hot water that loosened the hair so it could be scraped from the hide. The hog was then hung on a makeshift gallows for butchering, a process that wasted very little of the animal's flesh.

The liver was saved for stew; intestines for "chitlins" and sausage casing; ears and snout for souse; feet for pickling; and fat meat for lard, crackling bread, and seasoning. The skull, severed from the trunk on the cutting table, was cracked open for the brains, a choice delicacy; the backs and other chunks became pork chops and sausage. Finally the hams, shoulders, and side meat were packed in salt, where they remained for a couple of months before being cleaned and wired for hanging in the smokehouse.

The farmer's palate would not be satisfied until the best of the corn crop had been turned into hominy grits. This was accomplished by boiling the husks loose from the pulp with ashes or lye in an iron pot, then washing off the husks and cooking the pulp for hours to leave it tender. "And then, later on," in the words of a farm woman, "you cook your ham. And take out your hominy and heat that. Nothing better. Hominy and ham. Has a wonderful flavor. Hog and hominy."

The careworn sentinels of "hog and hominy" days still dot the countryside of rural North Carolina: old and decayed tobacco barns, the crumbling remains of livestock barns, hogpens, privies, the shells of abandoned dwelling houses. The livestock barn usually included a

central passageway that separated cow stalls on one side from mule or horse stalls on the other. But the gambrel roof also covered storage space for feed, tools, and machinery. Here cows were milked, horses shoed, equipment repaired, sick animals treated. But it was also the place where one might "pull up a bale of hay," as one farm lad recalled it, "just inside the door during a rainstorm and listen to the rain on the roof while you communicated with your soul." It was where children played hide-and-seek or performed rafter acrobatics with the hay as a cushion against any mishap, where dignity was recovered after a personal setback, and, like as not, where love was made.

Tobacco barn, Person County. Howard W. Odum Subregional Photo Study. The placard says: "It pays to sell your tobacco in Roxboro—Good Prices—Royal Welcome."

"It's amazing how many tobacco barns you see when you drive through the Carolinas. There's several sitting around every house. Looks like everybody there must be a tobacco farmer." Barefoot and Kornegay, *Mules and Memories*.

9

The "Cottontots"

Sharecropper's house, Chatham County, ca. 1938. Howard W. Odum Subregional Photo Study.

Mrs. Jim Jeffcoat summed up their situation: "We have never owned a horse or a mule or a cow or any tools or anything to ride in. Of course, we ain't never owned a house, and we never will. The house we've lived in ain't worth owning. They ain't worth nothing to nobody except to furnish pore croppers like us who can't do no better." Terrill and Hirsch, *Such as Us.*

Frances Carson remembers her childhood: "Papa was a farmer and he made us work so hard that we didn't go to school half of the time. We had to stay at home in the fall and grade 'backer and pick cotton, and in the spring we had to stay out to plant it. That's why I never got out of the fifth grade." Terrill and Hirsch, *Such as Us.*

Such reverie was likely to be a heritage of the life-style associated in the interwar years with farm ownership. But a third of North Carolina's white farmers and two-thirds of the black were tenants, mostly sharecroppers. Tenantry, in fact, was still expanding, and the average size of a North Carolina farm was still declining. As late as 1954, tenants comprised well over a third of all the state's farm families, and the average size of a Tar Heel farm—sixty-eight acres—was the smallest in the United States. Socially, tenantry was a system that may have saved the lives of the former slaves and impoverished whites who had sprung from the ruin of the Civil War. Economically, however, the system was a disaster, fostering a gulf between occupancy and ownership—between labor and its rewards—that wasted some of the country's best farmland.

Not for the typical tenant did the future hold romantic memories of "hog and hominy days." Tenant farmers owned little or no livestock and thus had no need for barns or other outbuildings. Most of them occupied farms too small for anything but total concentration on one or two cash crops. Most tenants were doomed by the long agricultural depression of those years to flee eventually to cities in search of employment. Only a few of them would achieve farm ownership. Tenants, sharecroppers especially, made up a class of itinerant poor who were buffeted from one meager farm to the next, living only for the day or the season. "It's a rare thing to find a sharecropper that's thrifty and saving," declared a Northampton County landlord. "The white ones as a rule ain't no better than the niggers. They're usually the slums of the world. . . . If 'twasn't for we landlords, what in God's world would become of this shiftless crowd?"

A study of 351 black and white families in northeastern Chatham County in 1923 showed rural life, tenant farming in particular, to be bleak to the point of despair. Almost half the families studied were tenants. Average daily income for a member of a sharecropping family was 9 cents; for a member of the relatively comfortable farm-owning family, 33 cents. Most tenants lived in unpainted frame houses at least thirty years old. None had running water, and only eight enjoyed the luxury of an outdoor privy. "The bushes and barn lot buildings," the report noted, "are the screens of family privacy for thirty houses." The study enumerated 203 missing windowpanes in various tenant homes, in many of which "it is possible to study astronomy through the holes in the roof and geology through the cracks in the floor."

Most tenant wives worked alongside their husbands in the fields eight to ten hours a day for up to seven months a year. At age seven or eight, boys and girls joined the farm labor force for all but six

10

Sharecroppers and their log cabin, ca. 1938. Howard W. Odum Subregional Photo Study.

"Tenants ain't got no chance. I don't know who gets the money, but it ain't the poor. It gets worse every year—the land gets more wore out, the prices for tobacco gets lower, and everything you got to buy gets higher. Like I told you, I'm trying to 'be content' like the Bible says and not to worry, but I don't see no hope." Hagood, *Mothers of the South.*

months of the school year. Doctors were visited or called only when all else failed. Nearly one infant in four was stillborn or died before age six. None of the tenant children had ever been vaccinated for typhoid or smallpox.

Apart from one two-year high school, this corner of Chatham County offered education in the form of six old, weather-stained, one-teacher schools. The teachers were mostly teen-aged girls and women, none of them a college graduate. Illiteracy among tenants ran close to 10 percent, and most children were finished with formal education by the end of the fifth or sixth grade. One tenant family in four subscribed to a newspaper; books and periodicals were rare.

The unrivaled community focus in northeastern Chatham was the church. All the church buildings had been painted at least "once upon a time" and were kept clean and in good repair. Most of the preachers were nonresidents who visited their flocks one Sunday a month; thus, most churchgoers alternated Sundays among several churches and denominations. The signal event of the year was the revival or "protracted meeting," which followed the autumn harvest. During such meetings "[e]ven the bootleggers fringed the outskirts

Lawrence School, near Corinth, Chatham County, ca. 1911, still standing though unused. North Carolina Collection, Louis R. Wilson Library, University of North Carolina, Chapel Hill.

Bellview schoolhouse, ca. 1917, now on the Moore County Board of Education grounds, U.S. #1 south of Sanford, once served a black community. It is authentically restored and furnished for use by every fourth-grade class one day a year.

Country church on "meeting" Sunday, Person County, 1938. Howard W. Odum Subregional Photo Study. Though built before 1920, the following churches are typical of those used in this period: Shiloh Church (no longer used), Penny Hill, on Tar River at Edgecombe-Pitt county line; Chapel of the Good Shepherd, Ridgeway vicinity, Warren County; and Pleasant Green Church, near Cole Mill Rd., Orange County.

of the crowds and . . . plied their trades." But sharecroppers often belonged to no church owing to their inability to read the hymns or contribute to the collection boxes.

The country store, like the church, was destined to retain well into the jet age its role as an important institution. When bad weather prohibited work in the fields, the tenant and landlord alike rode or walked to the general store. Here, swatting flies in summer or huddled around a potbellied stove in winter, the men of rural Chatham learned from one another and shared the little they knew of the world beyond. Often they brought in some eggs or chicken or beeswax to swap for supplies, and the storekeeper was obliged to keep a little of everything on hand. On leaving, they would carry away as much salt, sugar, snuff, chewing tobacco, coffee, and whiskey as their produce would bring in trade and whatever combs, shoes, paregoric, nails, axheads, or ready-made clothes their feeble credit would allow.

Cotton and tobacco were the principal crops, accounting for over half of North Carolina's farm income. These crops were a boon to small farmers because nearly all the work involved in production was done by hand and did not suffer from competition with mechanized neighbors. In fact, little real progress was made in mechanizing either crop before the decade of the 1950s.

Tobacco and cotton were grown throughout much of the state, and by the 1920s North Carolina had the largest tobacco and second largest textile industry in the nation. But heavy concentration on non-

Photograph by Bayard Wooten. N.C. State Archives.

Pope and Airy Store, Salisbury, Rowan County, renovated in 1938, still sells a bit of everything. Patterson's Mill Country Store, Farrington Rd., Durham County, recreates an old-time general store.

Prospect Hill general store, Caswell County, 1940. Howard W. Odum Sub-regional Photo Study.

A guided tour of Duke Homestead, Durham, Durham County, includes a grading bench and an explanation of all the steps in tobacco production from seedbed to market.

Grading bench, Granville County, 1938. Howard W. Odum Subregional Photo Study.

food crops lay at the root of the central paradox of the time: North Carolina, despite its devotion to agriculture, was a heavy importer of food. Much of what might have been profit was absorbed in the purchase of food and feed that could have been produced cheaply and in abundance at home. Dependence on nonfood crops also meant that farmers had ready money only for a while after a harvest and lived on credit the rest of the year.

Harvesting cotton involved the brutal labor of stooping and bending for every fluff of the fiber. No genius had done for picking cotton what Eli Whitney did for removing the seeds over a century before. Ginned cotton that had brought 35 cents a pound in 1919 commanded less than 6 cents in 1931. Global overproduction brought a sharp decline in cotton acreage after the mid-1920s, and "King Cotton" abdicated in favor of Duke Tobacco.

Flue-cured tobacco was produced in several sections of the state, while burley was confined to the Mountain region. Farmers who had been unable to keep up with wartime demand, however, found that they had grossly overproduced tobacco in 1920. As with cotton, prices fell until the leaf in 1932 brought only about a sixth of what it had fetched in 1919. Federally imposed allotments helped to achieve a gradual recovery for cotton and tobacco after 1934, but it was a long time before farmers felt adequately rewarded for the work involved in producing these crops.

The work of cultivating, harvesting, and curing tobacco was an eighteen-hour-a-day ordeal. Seeds planted in a cloth- or mulch-covered bed for about two months were transplanted into rows that had to be repeatedly cultivated to loosen the soil and keep out weeds. When the plant bloomed, the bloom was cut off to allow the upper leaves to develop. This "topping," like "suckering" (removing lateral shoots) and "priming" (picking the leaves as they ripen), was also hand labor. The leaves, often up to a hundred and fifty thousand to an acre, were than sledded to the barn, strung in bunches on sticks, and hung on racks for curing.

Tobacco barns had to be tight enough to seal in the high curing temperatures achieved by the furnace in the wall or under the floor. Pipes (or flues) circulated hot air that yellowed the leaves, killed the stems to prevent juice from running out, and, finally, dried the leaves. It all required round-the-clock vigilance for several days to keep the heat at proper levels and prevent an accident that could destroy in a few minutes the income of a season. Only after the dried leaves were graded (sorted by quality), tied in bundles, and packed, were they ready for market.

A dismayed observer emerged from his Chatham sojourn with misgivings over the role and fate of the sharecroppers, whose lives were bound so closely to this unremitting regimen. "They lack abiding citizenship," was his somber estimate, "and a sense of proprietary interest in schools and churches and neighborhood enterprises. They lack a sense of responsibility for community morals [and] . . . are widely tempted into the business of making and vending illicit liquors." But it was manifestly unfair to blame the patient for the disease, even to the extent that such judgments were fair-minded.

Indeed, Prohibition, which became law in North Carolina in 1909 and nationally in 1920, sometimes seemed specifically designed to help the rural poor survive the travails of prolonged depression. Unlike the raising of livestock or poultry, moonshining required little capital—at least when undertaken on a modest scale as a community service. "I've seen fathers take little kids five and six years old with 'em to the still," claimed a Prohibition-era sheriff. "And they just growed up in it; they didn't think there was anything wrong with it. That was their family business." The manufacture of illicit whiskey

Grading was a sociable task; women enjoyed the work. One explained: "Men ain't no good in 'bacca. They can't set still and work steady. They's always got to be goin' outdoors to see about somp'n—even if they ain't got no excuse better'n the dog." Hagood, *Mothers of the South*.

A bootlegger of Duplin County told how "In the days past, it was when I was quite a young man, I more or less kept my work a secret. I'd go to bed early 'n crawl out the window, work, makin' likker all night, an' then I'd slip back in 'fore the chickens crowed for day. . . . Kept a drunk around so's he could test it. If it didn't kill 'im, why, I could put it on the market. Didn't never kill one tester, not outright." Wolcott, *Rose Hill*.

15

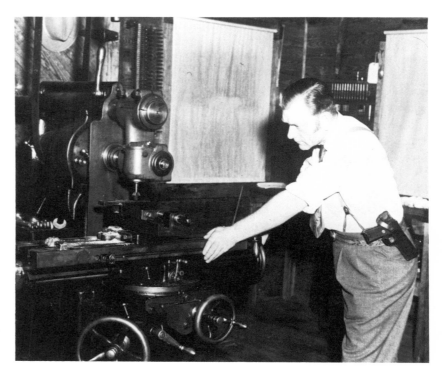

David ("Carbine") M. Williams, a genius with firearms, operating a milling machine in his shop near Godwin, Cumberland County. N.C. State Archives. This shop is now in the Museum of History, Raleigh, as part of a firearms display, which includes many of his inventions. His most famous was the .30 caliber M1 semiautomatic carbine developed for United States Army use in World War II.

was the mainstay of many a Chatham County family, though perhaps not on quite so grand a scale as in neighboring Orange, one of the state's premier moonshining counties.

Corn mash fermented with sugar, steamed in a boiler, and condensed through copper tubing could produce an agreeable whiskey. Apples, peaches, rye, wheat, barley, potatoes, and many other crops likewise yielded valuable alcoholic potions. A bushel of mash and a hundred pounds of sugar made eleven gallons of high-proof, tax-free whiskey that could mean the difference between failure for a season and breaking even—or perhaps even a small profit.

Hazards there were as in cotton and tobacco production. The heads and tails of the brew contained poisonous aldehydes and fusel oil. Any liquor distilled through lead coils instead of copper could cause lead poisoning. And then there was the sheriff or federal revenue agent. Implication in the death of one such officer at a still caused David Marshall ("Carbine") Williams, the most gifted Tar Heel inventor of the epoch, to spend much of his life in prison.

Prohibition's end in 1933 reduced but by no means curtailed moonshining and bootlegging. Huge road-building programs and the popularity of the automobile after World War II laced the state with innumerable Thunder Roads, along which prospective Junior Johnsons pitted their rum-running skills against the minions of the law. Progress often brought two headaches for every aspirin tablet.

Clarence Poe (1881–1953). N.C. State Archives.

The Case for Interdependence

Some analysts simply wrote off the small farmer as a doomed species. Clarence Poe, a Chatham County native and product of a one-room school there, followed the drift of the times in this regard. After becoming editor of the *Progressive Farmer*, an agricultural newspaper in Raleigh, in 1899, he built it into one of the great mass-circulation farm journals in the world. But Poe's editorials, perhaps reflecting his experience with small-farm America while coming of age in Chatham, evolved in favor of the large farmer, the most cost-efficient unit. It seemed useless, after all, to preach of tractors and combines to those for whom a good mule was still a status symbol; fruitless to sing the praises of indoor plumbing to those not able to own backyard privies.

17

Jane S. McKimmon (1867–1957), painted by Henry Rood, Jr., in 1947. North Carolina State University (NCSU) Archives. Mrs. McKimmon, appointed in 1911 to provide statewide demonstration work, expanded the work of the few canning clubs started by the Farmers' Cooperative Demonstration Work to every county of the state. These clubs taught women how to provide food year-round for their households and earn additional income with the surplus, how to grade and package eggs and vegetables, how to bake bread, and how to beautify their homes through sewing and handcrafts.

Egg-packers. NCSU Archives.

Other authorities felt they saw a possible salvation for the small farmer but were puzzled as to how it might be achieved. Farmers, one sociologist observed, "can not or will not act together in group production, group processing, group credit, and self-defensive group action in farm policies. . . . In the lonely life of isolated farms, there is developed an economic and social inertia that is stubbornly resistant to change of any sort." Another sociologist felt that "farmers are bred to think privately and locally in terms of the family and the neighborhood. They do not easily think in terms of the community and the commonwealth. The private-local mind of the farmer in the South is the ultimate obstacle to country community life and cooperative enterprise."

Experience demonstrated the persistence of the provincialism and individualism that lay at the core of the problem. The severe crash in farm prices in 1920 spawned marketing co-ops among cotton, tobacco, and peanut farmers, but only the cotton co-op survived beyond 1925. The Farmers' Union, chartered in North Carolina in 1905, was moribund by the late 1920s. But these were statewide and interstate experiments, and some strictly local co-ops survived, publicizing improved techniques and enabling their members to buy cheaper supplies. The modest success of these small enterprises in turn helped some farmers to overcome their suspicions of cooperative efforts.

A more effective mode of interdependence in the 1920s, however, was that facilitated by what is now the Agricultural Extension Service. This service was jointly created in 1909 by the State Agricultural and Mechanical College at Raleigh (now North Carolina State University) and the U.S. Department of Agriculture. By 1923 the extension service had "county agents" in three quarters of the state's one hundred counties. Most counties also had female demonstration agents who promoted rural home improvement. Boys' Corn Clubs and Girls' Canning Clubs (later known as 4-H clubs) were extension groups that paralleled the adult programs.

Extension agents popularized better ways of preparing, cultivating, and fertilizing crops. They encouraged wiser seed selection and drainage; improved livestock production; crop rotation; the organization of cooperative credit unions; and modern ideas of hygiene, diet, and sanitation. The agents also kept farmers abreast of the findings of the Agricultural Experiment Stations operated by State College.

The depression of 1929 generated a sense of catastrophe against which the trials of preceding years paled to insignificance. The market collapse cut farm income by 60 percent, and farmers reared to detect Old World tyranny in any formal organization found themselves listening attentively to the firebrands of regimentation. The Grange, defunct in North Carolina since the late nineteenth century, fluttered back to life in 1929 under the inspiration of Clarence Poe. Behind the leadership of Alamance County dairy farmer Kerr Scott, it tried to channel the frustration of farmers. By 1933 it had 12,500 members and claimed success in procuring such legislative relief as tax cuts and steps toward rural electrification. But farmers soon began deserting the Grange, perhaps impatient with its penchant for long-range remedies in the face of imminent disaster.

Increasingly, farmers looked to quicker solutions, and cooperation often seemed to be the answer. The statewide Farmers' Cooperative Exchange and the Central Carolina Cooperative Exchange in the upper Piedmont were two among many such groups formed in the early 1930s. They offered facilities for the cooperative purchase of fertilizers, feeds, seeds, and other supplies; promoted cooperative marketing; and stimulated interest in grading and other marketing fundamentals. The success of these efforts pointed up the growing acceptance among some farmers of the philosophy of common effort and foretold a time when scores of co-ops would serve the interests of farmers in hundreds of ways. "During the 1933–1936 period," one publication rhapsodized, "North Carolina farmers have learned more about cooperation than they had in the entire history of the State."

But co-ops by themselves were no cure-all for the problems of farming. Tobacco farmers, for example, experimented in the early 1920s with the Tri-State Growers' Cooperative. Members turned over their tobacco to the co-op, which graded, redried, and stored it until the best time for marketing. But farmers proved wary of the scheme and the Tri-State never gained enough control of the crop to create the monopoly it needed. Tri-State folded by 1926. A similar fate met efforts of the Federal Farm Board to organize a tobacco cooperative between 1929 and 1931.

Reacting in time-honored fashion to the emergency of the Great Depression, farmers increased production of their cash crops. This

Farmers' markets were an outgrowth of Mrs. McKimmon's program. The curb market, 221 N. Church St., Hendersonville, Henderson County, began on the sidewalk in 1924, but since 1954 it has had its own building in which to sell flowers, crafts, and food.

Margaret Hood Caldwell, Master of North Carolina State Grange, 1946–47 and 1963–75. Courtesy Mrs. Caldwell.

Schley Grange, Orange County, won a national contest in 1948 for its community program and received a brick colonial revival building as the prize.

A farm family, Reddies River, Wilkes County, 1938. Stutz and Maxfield, "Tobacco Bag Stringing Operations."

19

had the effect of driving prices down still further. The agony of these years forced many of them out of business for good. It was an era that was to leave bitter memories of "the sweat of an entire crop," as a Tar Heel recalled it, "with nothing in hand at the end to show for their labors; walking everywhere . . . because there was either no gas or no car; swapping eggs for absolute necessities at a penny apiece; working (when any work was available) at five cents an hour, and getting paid in anything but money."

Roosevelt's New Deal provided many rural North Carolinians with a cushion against the fall that could not be prevented. In tobacco, the result was little short of startling. When the Agricultural Adjustment Administration (AAA) signaled its receptivity to the ideas of farmers in 1933, tobacco men responded with scores of local and mass meetings. They proposed that the AAA find some means of limiting production so as to raise prices. This was accomplished through a contract system that pushed prices from 11.6 cents a pound in 1932 to 15.3 cents in 1933, and added over $50 million in that year to the income of tobacco growers.

Given the political realities of the epoch, it was perhaps inevitable that this and similar programs aided the well-to-do farmer far more than the poor one. "The government farm program hasn't helped me much," declared a Northampton County landlord in 1939.

Diana Morgan as a child would visit the family laundress now and then: "She was always gracious and would invite me in. She never apologized for the way anything looked. I thought to myself at the time: How odd that Caroline uses newspaper to paper walls. I didn't have any brains at eleven or twelve or whatever to think: what kind of country is this that lets people live in houses like this and necessitates their using the Sunday paper for wallpaper!" Terkel, *Hard Times*.

House on poor land, 1936, Bladen County. NCSU Archives.

"Some big farmers profited by it. . . . All I drawed last year for co-opin' with the government was $25, and half of that went to the sharecroppers." Tenants who made the acreage and crop reductions encouraged by the government often received nothing for their trouble, the landlord simply pocketing the federal checks without sharing them. On the whole, however, the system worked and complaints never reached serious proportions.

Other federal programs, such as the Rural Electrification Authority (REA), would ultimately play key roles in raising rural living standards. But farmers and other North Carolinians remained on the whole suspicious of the bureaucrat bearing gifts and yielded to federal initiatives with misgivings. Tar Heel congressmen who warmly endorsed the federal tobacco program raised the cry of socialism against parallel ventures in behalf of the cash crops of other sections of the country or for the relief of distressed elements such as the urban poor. "The economic emergency of the 1930s," concludes a recent study of the tobacco program, "failed to shift traditions of individualism and business hostility to federal intervention."

The Guns of Deliverance

No measure of relief or cooperation could replace the stimulus of a resurgent economy and demand for farm produce, and this was the achievement of Adolf Hitler more than Roosevelt and the New Dealers. An agricultural boom was touched off by World War II, bringing economic blessings destined to rescue North Carolina farms from the blight of preceding decades. Wartime military and industrial demands drew off hordes of young men, including hundreds of farmers. Scarce agricultural labor forced many farmers to acquire tractors and other machines they might otherwise have resisted buying. Returning veterans were offered educational opportunities that would soon be translated into improved farms and higher living standards.

The war's end, however, found North Carolina still agriculturally backward in comparison with many other parts of the country. One farm in seven had running water; telephones were rare, mules abundant. Much corn and other grain was still imported, but the state was in the midst of enormous changes.

Farms began increasing in size during the 1950s, making feasible the use of heavy machinery. Corn pickers, hay bailers, grain combines, trucks, and tractors, often shared among a number of neighbors, came into general use. So did pesticides, herbicides, hybrid seeds, and much else. By the end of the 1950s, three farm families in four had automobiles, every other one had a freezer, and every third one a telephone.

Tenantry declined rapidly in the postwar era, spurred on by a black exodus after 1950. Cotton fell rapidly in importance, but North Carolina produced two thirds of the nation's flue-cured tobacco. The first transplanters and harvesters appeared in the tobacco fields, emancipating thousands from traditional drudgery. Farmers diversified production, turning to sweet potatoes, soybeans, beef, milk, turkeys, chickens, and eggs. By 1960 poultry that formerly went north for processing could be handled at the rate of three million birds a week in the state's processing plants. A diversified farm was one on which tractors and other equipment could be used year-round rather than merely from time to time. The most successful farmers were those who understood the new relationships between farming and the world of commerce and could transform themselves into agribusinessmen.

The encroachment of urban boundaries into the countryside and the rapid growth of transport facilities meant that many members of

Farming at Lake Mattamuskeet, Hyde County, 1930s. Photograph from the U.S. Department of the Interior. The largest natural lake on the East Coast, it covers thirty thousand acres. The rich, submerged soil has attracted drainage attempts since the 18th century. Drained, it yielded nine hundred bushels of sweet potatoes per acre; the national average was a hundred.

farm families could now take full- or part-time work off the farm. Farm income tended to improve with the availability of outside work, and the gulf that historically separated urban from rural life narrowed. Many who abandoned commercial farming were able to continue as part-time farmers who lived mainly on nonfarm incomes.

Food production so far outstripped population growth that farmers did not often enjoy the full reward of their new methods and technology. The standard of farm living, for all its progress, lagged well behind that of cities. Many farm homes of the 1960s lacked plumbing, complete kitchen facilities, and other conveniences. Farm income was much lower than urban, and rural areas usually lagged in availability of health care, educational quality, and other indexes of social advance. Offsetting such considerations was the reflection that rural America still enjoyed a relative freedom—from crime, pollution, and traffic—for which many an urbanite might gladly surrender some of his own benefits. In the flight to suburbia lay an admission that, for many Americans, country living had not lost its charm.

New patterns of ownership and operation emerged as farms became larger and more mechanized. Some farmers pooled their resources in corporate arrangements. Specialized operations, notably in dairying and poultry, became more common. And, in the 1960s and 1970s, there appeared in North Carolina the phenomenon of the "superfarm," perhaps the most exciting development of all.

The vast areas of swampland in eastern North Carolina had for more than a century tempted the imagination of agriculturalists. Beneath much of the wasteland lay some of the blackest, richest soil in the world, soil that could not fail to yield immense farming wealth if it could be cleared and drained. Moreover, such areas raised the possibility of eastern superfarms to rival those already pioneered in the Midwest. But a Tar Heel superfarm, much closer to northeastern population centers and European markets, seemed likely to surpass any profits dreamed of by remote midwesterners.

After several false starts in the vicinity of Lake Mattamuskeet in Hyde County, the 1920s saw the emergence of New Holland Farm, the state's initial superfarm. August Hecksher, a wealthy New Yorker, poured money into canals, ditches, and pumping plants to drain the lake, and brought in Dutch immigrants to do the work and a midwestern superfarmer to head the operation. A landscape architect laid out a town called New Holland. By 1933 the farm had fifty-one tractors, a thousand acres of rice, the world's largest soybean acreage, buckwheat, lespedeza, barley, celery, asparagus, rye, oats, flax, potatoes, and popcorn.

Neighboring small farms grumbled that the enterprise would not work and perhaps experienced some satisfaction over what happened in 1933. Failing pumps and attacks by regiments of armyworms, grasshoppers, and corn borers so devastated New Holland that Heck-

Another Dutch settlement began in 1925 at Terra Ceia, Beaufort County. A New York investment company tried to develop its holdings as farmland. The attempt failed, but the manager began to use the land for tulips and built a thriving business. A tulip festival with street dancing and big bands became an annual event in Washington, North Carolina, after 1937 until World War II.

Mattamuskeet Lodge when it was the pumping station for Hecksher's New Holland Farm experiment. Photograph from the U.S. Department of the Interior. The smokestack has been converted to an observation tower for the Wildlife Refuge, the present use of the lake and the surrounding land. It supports two hundred species of birds.

sher gave up. The multimillion-dollar investment was written off, and North Carolina's first superfarm ended in disaster.

But Hecksher's experiment was more nearly the beginning of the superfarm concept than the end. Several similar operations were opened in the northeastern section of the state during the 1960s and 1970s. First Colony Farms, the brainchild of former Winston-Salem trucking executive Malcolm McLean, was the most ambitious of these. When First Colony began operating in 1973, it encompassed over three hundred and fifty thousand acres in four counties. McLean envisioned an enterprise that within a few years would produce a million hogs and a hundred thousand head of cattle a year. First Colony Farms was the largest privately owned, single-unit farm in the United States, but whether it was destined to become the century's agricultural miracle or debacle could not be foretold.

24

Epilogue

By 1973 highways 64 and 15-501 sped traffic through Chatham County past towering silos and long rows of poultry houses. Here was vivid evidence of the changes that had brought higher standards of living to nearly every farm family. But the driver who turned off the main routes, who paused for a fill-up or a Coke at Bynum or Farrington, still found long stretches of country whose appearance had changed but little in fifty years.

The log cabin and the two-room shanty were still to be seen here and there along the back ways, though rapidly giving way to the brick cottage or mobile home. The country church and crossroads general store survived, though there were fewer of the latter than in earlier times. Abandoned houses, boarded-up businesses, and fields gone to weeds testified to the migration that had taken so many away from farming. Yet, the county was still heavily rural and was in some respects still geared to the rhythms of earlier times.

But Chatham was now also the third largest livestock and poultry county in the state. The resident of the wooded back road was often a mill hand in industrial Durham or a clerk at the university town, Chapel Hill. If he farmed at all, it was likely to be some form of subsistence gardening. Recreational opportunities had expanded mightily for him, and there was talk of an immense reservoir to be built by the U.S. Army Corps of Engineers that would bring vacationers to Chatham in droves. A TV antenna jutted from Chatham's rooftop, water and sewer pipes stretched beneath its floor, a car waited in its driveway. Health care was readily accessible, and educational opportunity had expanded powerfully. If Chatham's taste craved heartier fare than TV or movies, the arts and sciences beckoned from Duke and Chapel Hill.

The age of agribusiness left little room for the rugged individualist. The giant corporation's access to credit, influence with government, and links with national food chains gave it enormous power. Small or large, farmers had little choice but to contract with a corporation. Farming was now seen as a link in the chain of production that ran from the factory and laboratory to the consumer's refrigerator and linen closet. Whether agribusiness produced better food or reasonable prices or a fair return for the producer became matters for heated debate.

Family in front of unfinished house. NCSU Archives. Air-conditioning and a TV aerial will replace the amenities of the old house: a porch and a chimney.

25

The Electric Cornucopia

The Big Three

Although North Carolina in 1920 might with ample justice have been called an agricultural state, by far the larger part of its wealth at this time came from manufacturing. The leading industries, each thriving on cheap labor and the local availability of raw materials, were tobacco, cotton textiles, and furniture. In the preceding twenty years, North Carolina had advanced from twenty-seventh to fifteenth among all the states in the value of manufactured articles. During the 1920s, it would become the leading industrial state in the Southeast. In this rapid advance lay the source of both the pride and the heartbreak of the Old North State.

The three major industries were largely concentrated in an area roughly the shape of a reaping hook. The tip of this configuration lay in Raleigh, the blade curving west and southwest along the route of the Southern Railway through Durham, Greensboro, and Winston-Salem to Charlotte. The handle stretched westward from Charlotte, paralleling the South Carolina border to Rutherford County. In this Piedmont region were concentrated most of the main population centers of North Carolina.

Manufacturing was by 1920 a billion-dollar-a-year activity in North Carolina, which ranked second only to Texas in the South. Drawing heavily on tenants leaving or being driven from farms, the state's industrial enterprises employed more than a hundred and sixty thousand people in some six hundred plants from the mountains to the sea. Other than the Big Three, the chief Tar Heel industries were pulp and paper, lumber, fertilizer, flour and meal, cottonseed oil, leather, railway car construction and repair, and publishing and printing. But all the lesser industries combined produced only a third of the wealth of the larger three.

The dominant power source for the major manufacturers was the Southern (later Duke) Power Company, established in 1904 by tobacco magnate James B. ("Buck") Duke. Other producers of electric power (Carolina Power and Light in the East, Tallassee in the West) served the state, but Southern controlled the industrial Piedmont, supplying energy from its hydroelectric stations on the Catawba River.

The tobacco industry was almost wholly contained within three cities in the same small area of the northern Piedmont: R. J. Reynolds at Winston-Salem, Liggett and Myers at Durham, and the

(Opposite) Power generators at Fontana Dam, Graham County. Part of the TVA system and the Appalachian Trail, the dam is 480 feet high (highest in the eastern United States). In 1945, when the dam was completed, the construction village was converted into a resort.

American Tobacco Company at Durham and Reidsville. The great growth of this industry in North Carolina had occurred largely since 1913 and was the result of the burgeoning popularity of the cigarette. An urban society that recoiled from snuff and chewing tobacco and was often too fastidious for pipes and cigars found in the cigarette the ideal form of smoking. Even women and girls of the flapper generation felt comfortable with the cigarette, which was handy to carry, less messy than rival articles, inexpensive, and, to the taste not accustomed to stronger fare, satisfying. Each of the three most popular brands introduced since 1913—Camels, Chesterfields, and Lucky Strikes—was made in North Carolina, Camels exclusively so.

Reynolds was producing 30 billion Camels a year before the end of the 1920s and easily outpaced every other brand in the world. American began to counterattack strongly in 1923 with an advertising campaign that featured the skywriting of "Lucky Strikes" over 122 cities. Soon, diet-conscious consumers were being advised to "Reach for a *Lucky* instead of a sweet," and in 1929 Lucky Strike soared past Camel as the most popular cigarette. Four years later, the Liggett and Myers entry, Chesterfield, also passed Camels. Reynolds in 1934 put over 80 percent of its net revenue into advertising in an effort to regain Camel's priority. Famous personalities like Bill Tilden and Carl Hubbell were hired for testimonials, and a 3,000-square-foot electric "Camel" sign was raised over Times Square and 42nd Street. As a result, Camels were back on top in 1935 and would stay there until after World War II.

Sophisticated equipment in North Carolina factories shot out cigarettes at machine-gun rates to keep pace with the international demand. The state's thirty-odd tobacco factories manufactured a quarter of all the leaf in the United States, and the proportion would soon reach and then surpass a half. Primarily because of booming cigarette sales, North Carolina paid the federal government more in taxes than all but four other states. Moreover, the cigarette business would continue to expand through the bleakest days of the depression as American consumption more than doubled between 1927 and 1939. Cigars, chewing tobacco, and snuff declined in use during the interwar years, though cigars would make a rally during the 1930s.

So thoroughly was the cigarette industry automated that relatively few laborers were employed in it. Most of the work force was employed in stemmeries and redrying plants where the workers were mostly unskilled, black, and poorly paid. Though there were many indirect benefits of so large an industry in North Carolina, tobacco manufacture was of little direct help to the state's employment problems.

Employing only a tenth of the state's industrial labor force in 1929, the three main tobacco firms produced more than a third of the value of North Carolina's manufactures.

A swelling national population that demanded huge amounts of housing and furnishings provided the impetus for the surging growth of North Carolina's furniture industry. What was needed to meet the demand was a vast pool of unskilled labor and virtually inexhaustible supplies of various hardwoods, both of which western North Carolina could readily furnish. In addition, the heritage of the western region included a tradition of skilled cabinetmaking brought over in earlier times by West European craftsmen. But it was the post-World War I housing boom that fueled the great new phase of the furniture industry's expansion after 1920.

This postwar development was experienced mainly in the opening of new shops and plants. Technology in the furniture business improved only slowly, perhaps because of the strong craft roots of the industry. Gradually, however, manufacturing techniques were improved, factory layout was made more efficient, and scientific methods of control were introduced into the wood-drying process, the key production bottleneck. The wider use of waterproof resins and improved finishing processes, along with the adoption of conveyor systems, stepped up production dramatically during the late 1930s and 1940s. By 1939 North Carolina was manufacturing more wooden household furniture than any other state and ranked first in dining-room and bedroom furniture, fifth in kitchen furniture, and eighth in living-room and library furniture. Much of the industry's progress was the consequence of the role of the Southern Furniture Exposition Building, erected at High Point in 1921 as a stimulus to design and sales. The annual market at the building was soon the largest in the South. By 1947 the building could display six acres of furniture on its fourteen floors. Buyers from forty-eight states and many foreign countries—five thousand of them in that year—swarmed through the building to examine the new lines and place their orders. No other economic event was so important to North Carolina.

Furniture-making also fostered the growth of related industries. Every new chair or bedstead sold was cash in the pockets of loggers and lumbermen. It meant profit for the makers of boxes and containers, veneers, and finishing materials. Upholsterers used quantities of cotton batting and materials from Tar Heel textile plants. The furniture industry gave incentive to the producers of paints, hardware, springs, glue, and resins. On furniture's steady currents were carried flotillas of business enterprise.

Furniture-making, like the other major industries of North Carolina, was not simply supplying a recognized need. Consumerism by the 1920s was already a flourishing psychological science complete with laboratories and instructional manuals. Some of the nation's best brains were occupied in the study of how to stimulate consumption, how to give life's furbelows the appearance of necessities. Through-

Most North Carolina furniture companies are family-owned, such as the Broyhills' Lenoir Furniture Company, the Finches' Thomasville Chair Company, the Tates' and Holdens' Continental Furniture Company at High Point, and the Whites' furniture company at Mebane.

29

30

out the state and nation, values and tastes were being gradually nationalized and urbanized. The movies and media advertising helped to create a sense of inadequacy among those who had not yet tied into electric and sewer lines. Interior decor took on the dimensions of an important art form.

Rags and Riches

Textiles ranked first among the leading industries of North Carolina. There were seven hundred mills within a radius of a hundred miles of Charlotte, and others scattered across the state.

By 1920 North Carolina boasted the world's largest mills for the manufacture of hosiery (Durham), towels (Kannapolis), denim (Greensboro), damask (Roanoke Rapids), and underwear (Winston-Salem). Eighty-five percent of the nation's combed yarn—used primarily in the more expensive types of women's wear—was made in Gaston County's one hundred mills. But much of this productivity was a response to inflated wartime demands, and the decade of the 1920s brought a gradual decline in the per capita consumption of textiles. Intense competition among thousands of small firms scattered all across the state also had adverse effects on the industry, which, like farming, entered the Great Depression in poor condition to cope with it. For a time in the 1920s, tobacco replaced textiles as North Carolina's industrial leader.

But the textile industry had its entrepreneurial geniuses who not only coped but also prospered even in the darkest interwar years. Probably the outstanding textile manufacturer in North Carolina was J. Spencer Love of Burlington. The son of a Harvard mathematics professor, Love was graduated from Harvard in 1917, saw brief service in World War I, and afterward went to work as paymaster for a small textile firm in Gastonia. During the postwar recession, he was able to purchase the plant with his modest savings, only to be forced to auction off all but the machinery in 1923. With a business acumen seasoned by a keen interest in experimental fabrics and new technology, Love became a pioneer in the production of rayon, which gave Burlington its first big boost. By 1934 Burlington was the country's largest weaver of rayon fabrics. By the time of his death in 1962, Love had built Burlington Industries into the colossus of textile manufacturing; the company then operated 130 plants located in sixteen states and seven foreign countries. Shrewd innovation, sound management, and an ability to parry the thrusts of organized labor enabled Burlington to prosper in an arena where thousands of rivals had failed.

More than any other North Carolina industry, textiles fostered the concept of the mill village: a compact aggregation of houses

James Spencer Love (1896–1962). Photograph by Fabian Bachrach. Courtesy Burlington Industries. The son of North Carolinians, Love built up the largest and most diversified textile business in the world.

31

located in the vicinity of a mill, owned by the company, and rented to the workers. Like the feudal manor and antebellum plantation, the mill village fostered a suffocating paternalism that frustrated the efforts of labor organizers long after the owners surrendered control of the villages themselves. Although reformers not infrequently missed the point in decrying the manifest evils of these communities, these small frame dwellings usually represented a step up in life for those who resided in them. A family coming in from a leaky shanty of rural Chatham County, for example, might encounter in a mill village its first experience with electric lights and indoor plumbing. On the other hand, mill villagers sometimes took little interest in the appearance of their rented quarters. The result was that the mill village could become a squalid place, the resort of bootleggers and prostitutes.

Not every mill village could be described this way. Some mill owners practiced an enlightened form of paternalism that expressed itself in day-to-day concern for the welfare of the mill people. At Cramerton, in Gaston County, owner Stuart W. Cramer provided attractive houses set off by lawns, hedges, and flowers. He maintained a community center and golf course as well as a farm that furnished villagers with fresh eggs, milk, chickens, and vegetables. Pay scales and productivity were said to be higher at Cramerton than at most textile mills. There were also mill towns in which the residents took a keen interest in the appearance of their houses and the moral atmosphere of the community.

Most of the mill villages were sold to their occupants after the early 1930s as textile owners found them expensive to maintain and a burden to operate. An exception was Kannapolis, where owner

32

Charles A. Cannon clung doggedly to the village as it expanded into a town and small city. In 1970 Kannapolis was the largest unincorporated municipality in the United States, its inhabitants still without political influence in the governing of the town. Cannon's mild but eccentric paternalism embraced a program, launched in the 1930s, of rebuilding downtown Kannapolis in pseudo-Williamsburg style. At his death in 1971, Cannon owned only about a fifth of the housing, but he had built one of the world's great textile empires, with twenty-four thousand employees in North and South Carolina.

Even if most mill villages had company-owned schools, churches, and recreational facilities, the house rent of 50 cents a week per room could cut deeply into workers' wages, which were often as low as nine dollars a week or less. Mill town ministers identified their own fortunes, as well as those of their flocks, with the fortunes of mill owners and preached a gospel attuned almost exclusively to the Life Beyond. It was, in fact, the same gospel preached from many of the pulpits of rural Chatham County.

Fruit of the Loom

Organized labor could expect little encouragement in this setting. A spate of unsuccessful strikes in North Carolina at the turn of the century was apparently one reason why unionism languished in the state after World War I. But there were certain other reasons as well. Among these were the strong opposition of mill owners and the responsiveness of state government to the sentiments of the owners. There may also have been a residue of rural provincialism, individualism, and conservatism among the workers that militated against all forms of regimentation. This, at least, has long been suggested as part of the reason for the disorganization of labor in North Carolina. On the other hand, worker acceptance of factory labor was in itself a notable concession to regimentation.

A series of wage-cuts at the onset of the recession of 1920–21 brought a brief round of strikes, but Governor Cameron Morrison sent the National Guard to the strike centers, and the ardor of the unionizers quickly cooled. For most of the decade of the 1920s, the Tar Heel textile industry remained sluggish, and unionism in this and other industries remained minimal.

Textile men struggled to counter the business slump by layoffs, pay-cuts, and economies of operation. Such measures sometimes gave relief for the firms but tended also to aggravate the poor working conditions in the mills. Mill hands, a third of whom were women and children over fourteen years old, typically worked ten or eleven hours a day, fifty-five hours a week. The mills were thick with dust, cotton fibers, and an oppressive humidity that caused a high incidence

When mill houses were sold to individual owners, the village lost its homogeneity and the mill workers the stereotype that had dogged them. Mill worker Julius Fry explained that "the people that didn't work in the plant and who didn't live exactly on the village thought that they were better than we were . . . they weren't cotton millworkers, they weren't lint dodgers. . . . And there's just such a feeling of second class citizenship, because the people uptown were 'better' than we were." SOHP.

33

Women working in a North Carolina textile mill. North Carolina Collection. Zelma Murray, an Alamance County textile worker, reported: "We worked ten hours a day and five on Saturday. I worked fifty-five hours a week, and I drawed $11.55." SOHP.

of respiratory ills. "I had seen women," said a mill worker, "going all day in that unbearable heat with their clothes stuck to their bodies like they had been dipped in a pail of water. Going up and down the alleys weeping, working, all day long." The workers existed on grits, beans, bread, field peas, cornmeal, and fatback, which approximated the diet of the antebellum slave. Fruits and vegetables were rare; mortality rates were relatively high.

Loray Mill, Gastonia, Gaston County, now owned by the Firestone Company.

Mounting distress among workers found expression in a new rash of textile strikes in early 1929 in North and South Carolina and Tennessee. Most were spontaneous with no unions involved, but three of the four in North Carolina were organized by the National Textile Workers' Union (NTWU), a Communist-led group. Far and away the most serious strike was that of the Loray Mill in Gastonia, reputedly the largest factory in the world under one roof.

Gastonia was described in 1929 as "a pretty little Southern town" of some twenty thousand people. Most Loray workers were former mountaineers and sharecroppers who occupied the mill village just outside the town limits. The plant produced fabric for automobile tires and was struggling frantically against competition from manufacturers of balloon tires.

Loray's owners in 1927 hired an efficiency expert who raised production despite reducing the work force by almost half. Pay scales were cut to an average of about thirteen dollars a week and even lower for most women and the blacks who made up the custodial staff. But much of the expert's success lay in the introduction of the so-called "stretch-out" system, under which weavers were assigned additional looms to operate. This system was already in use in the Cone textile mills in Greensboro and in other North Carolina plants.

The stretch-out was the source of prolonged and bitter complaints. "It used to be," as a Loray worker put it, "that you could git five, ten minutes rest now and then, so's you could bear the mill. But now you got to keep a-runnin' all the time. Never a minute to git your breath all day. I used to run six drawing frames and now I look after ten. You just kaint do it. A man's dead beat at night." "Hundreds of

Lacy Wright told what happened when the workers at Cone Mills tried to form a union: "And the company got on them people so bad about trying to organize down there that they fired I don't know how many of them, take their furniture and set it out in the streets, out of the mill houses and out in the streets. Wouldn't even let the people have time to find them another house and move into it." SOHP.

35

Ella May Wiggins, on the cover of a
labor periodical. North Carolina Collection. Mrs. Wiggins composed a ballad,
later sung at her funeral, on the plight of
women mill workers:

"We leave our children in the morning,
We kiss our children good-bye,
While we slave for the bosses,
Our children scream and cry.

. . . .

Now listen to me, Workers,
Both women and men,
We are sure to win our union,
If all would enter in."

Labor Defender, October 1929.

people," said another, "go to jail every year and spend the best part
of their lives there for doing things not half as harmful to their fellow
man as the stretch out."

The efficiency expert was replaced late in 1928, but by that time
it was too late to prevent the NTWU from obtaining a toehold at
Loray. The work force walked off the job in March 1929. They demanded twenty dollars for a five-day, forty-four-hour week, an end to
the 'stretch-out' system, equal pay for women, lower rent for mill
housing, improved sanitary conditions, and recognition of the union.
The arrival of radical agitators from New York and elsewhere alarmed
most of the workers and caused them to return to work in a few
days. But several hundred stayed on strike.

A history of sour relations between townsmen and mill people,
coupled with the presence of several Communists, created a volatile
situation in Gastonia. A police raid on union headquarters in June resulted in the killing of Gastonia's police chief and the subsequent mob-
demolition of the union headquarters and adjacent tent village. During
ensuing weeks, a union sympathizer was kidnapped and beaten, an
English journalist was assaulted, two graduate students were run
out of town, and fires broke out mysteriously in many places. In
September a truckload of strikers was attacked outside Gastonia and
a passenger, Ella May Wiggins, was killed. Several strikers were
convicted in the death of the police chief, but no one in that of
Mrs. Wiggins.

Organized labor in North Carolina was dealt a setback of incal-
culable dimensions by the events of 1929 in Gastonia. The mutual
antipathy of townsmen and workers there was not uncommon in
industrial centers, and the memory of the strife is still a sore one in
Gaston County. The National Guard, which was sent to Gastonia by
Governor O. Max Gardner (himself a mill owner), appeared to some
to be there to protect the mill and other property. Thereafter, the
specter of Communism was raised against every serious strike in
North Carolina. The Loray plant, now under different management,
still has no union.

Sporadic strikes have marked the history of North Carolina's
textile industry since 1929. Wage-cuts and poor working conditions
brought cotton mill strikes at High Point, Rockingham, and elsewhere
in 1932. Nearly a hundred North Carolina mills joined the general
strike of 1934. Burlington's J. Spencer Love was not speaking for
himself alone when he told *Forbes* magazine that unions were "funda-
mentally unsound." This was because "to live they must promote
strife, distrust, and discontent and set employee against employee,
class against class, and group against group."

Unionism received a boost when the right of collective bargain-
ing was recognized in the National Industrial Recovery Act (1933),
and in 1937 state laws further restricted the employment of children.

Working hours for females in industry were limited to forty-eight a week and nine a day, while male hours were reduced to fifty-five weekly and ten daily. But North Carolina, which ranked forty-seventh in 1939 in the percentage of its nonagricultural workers who were unionized, slipped later to forty-eighth and then found its seemingly permanent niche at fiftieth in the nation. "Folks can talk all they want about their right to join a union," as a disillusioned mill hand put it, "but right don't count much when money is against you."

While unions enjoyed some local victories during these years, some groups of workers continued to experience discrimination and hardship. Notably, the ten thousand or so migrant laborers who worked each year in North Carolina suffered from poor working conditions and lack of adequate legal protection. Women, in 1970 as in 1920, continued to experience the low wages that helped bring on the violence of 1929.

Affluence and Effluents

Ignited by the unprecedented demands of World War II, North Carolina industry in the 1940s entered upon an epoch of rapid expansion. A student of the subject in 1954 ranked the state as the South's industrial leader, one of the twelve foremost industrial states in the nation. The primary industries were still textiles, tobacco, and furniture, but the share of the first two in the state's overall industry was beginning to slip. Along with sawmills and related industries, the Big Three in 1954 accounted for almost half of North Carolina's manufacturing concerns. Already, as reported in the *North Carolina Almanac and Industrial Guide*, the state had two and one-half times more manufacturing concerns than it had had on the eve of the war. Substantial growth had occurred since 1939 in rubber, chemicals, electrical machinery, and other industries.

In textiles, the multiplication of spindles was replaced as the focus of development by the employment of more sophisticated machinery, by research aimed at the production of better yarns and fabrics, and by improved dyeing and finishing techniques. More North Carolinians were employed in textiles than in all other industries combined, but at wages still well below the national average. In its concern to keep textile prices and costs down by minimizing wages, the industry was beginning to move away from large urban areas and into the countryside, where competition for labor was less severe. The pressure of foreign competition was also taking a toll of anxiety among textile people.

North Carolina by the 1950s produced 40 percent of all the hosiery manufactured in the nation and led the South in woolens and worsteds. But the major new trend in textiles was the shift of the

northeastern apparel industry to North Carolina. Truck and highway facilities that brought Tar Heel mills within overnight proximity to the New York garment district were key factors in the shift. So was the availability in North Carolina of a large labor force of employable women, who ultimately comprised 85 percent of the apparel workers in North Carolina. But, even as they helped to perpetuate North Carolina's notoriety as a cheap-labor state, apparel plants sprouted in previously unindustrialized parts of the Mountain and Coastal Plain regions. Other industry followed apparel's lead, dispersing North Carolina industry from its traditional base in the Piedmont.

In the postwar era, as before, North Carolina remained the nation's leading tobacco manufacturer, producing more than half the country's smoking tobacco, snuff, and chewing tobacco. P. Lorillard of Greensboro, maker of Old Gold cigarettes, took its position in the 1950s beside Reynolds, Liggett and Myers, and American Tobacco as a tobacco giant. Pipe tobacco remained chiefly the province of the older three, while Brown and Williamson of Winston-Salem was the chief manufacturer of snuff. Greensboro's El Moro was the only leading brand of cigar produced in North Carolina.

Furniture's boom not only continued but accelerated, with output more than tripling between 1939 and 1957. Though the business was still centered largely in the Piedmont counties of Guilford, Davidson, Catawba, Burke, and Caldwell, plants were emerging as far east as Goldsboro and west to Waynesville. Two-thirds of all the furniture in the South was made within a hundred-and-fifty-mile radius of High Point; this area contained the greatest concentration of furniture factories in the world. Like textiles, furniture remained a labor-intensive, low-wage industry.

State government played an important role in the growth and dispersal of North Carolina industry, especially after Luther Hodges became governor in 1954. Hodges, a former textile manufacturer, rejuvenated the State Department of Conservation and Development and initiated a Building and Development Corporation to provide long-term capital for new and expanding industries. Hodges also sponsored tax concessions and an ambitious program of industry hunting, including missions to six nations of Western Europe. In the six years of his administration, the state gained over a thousand new plants and the expansion of more than fourteen hundred others.

Hodges would be best remembered for his work in launching the Research Triangle. The basic idea had been bandied about for several

IBM Building, Research Triangle Park, Durham County. Courtesy IBM Corporation. The original site, pictured here in 1966, has now been expanded to cover 2.7 million square feet.

Burroughs Wellcome Company, Research Triangle Park, Durham County. Courtesy of the company. Built in 1972 and designed by Paul Rudolph, the structure is an architectural achievement.

years, chiefly through the interest of social scientist Howard W. Odum at the University of North Carolina at Chapel Hill and Romeo H. Guest, head of a Greensboro contracting firm. Hodges became interested in the possibility of using the research capabilities of the three major universities at Raleigh, Chapel Hill, and Durham as a lure to bring corporate laboratories and research centers to North Carolina. Through private contributions, the Research Triangle Institute acquired funds with which to purchase a tract of four thousand acres of rural land lying within a "triangle" formed by the three schools. By 1959 the Research Triangle was a reality, its parks soon to be dotted with facilities representing Chemstrand, the U.S. Forest Service, IBM, Burroughs Wellcome, the U.S. Environmental Protection Agency, and many more. Even more dramatically than the adjacent urban complexes, the Triangle Park sprouted glacial monoliths of steel and glass to soar above the embracing glades and pastures. Piedmont farming communities within the Triangle found themselves abruptly cheek-by-jowl with enclaves of Ph.D.'s and aerospace engineers. The twentieth century seemed almost to have been bypassed in a headlong plunge from the nineteenth century into the twenty-first.

The scope of industry's problems grew apace with the scale of manufacturing enterprise during the 1950s and 1960s. The mining industry avoided a recurrence of the Coal Glen disaster of 1925, during which sixty men died in an explosion near Sanford, but North Carolina still had major mining interests as the leading producer of feldspar and mica as well as large quantities of talc and other minerals. Continuing tension between industry and labor was underscored by troubles at the Harriet-Henderson Cotton Mills at Henderson in the 1950s, the Roanoke Rapids plant of the J. P. Stevens textile firm, and elsewhere.

With industrial growth came industrial waste. The valuable commercial fishing industry began to feel the effects of chemical pollutants, which damaged the rich shellfish grounds along the coast. Areas of scenic beauty and archeological significance could not always be defended against the consequences of urban and industrial sprawl.

By the close of the 1960s, North Carolina's industry represented over 14 percent of that of the entire South and almost 4 percent of that of the United States. Food processing, metalworking, chemicals, electrical and nonelectrical equipment, instruments, rubber and plastics, stone, clay and glass, and transport equipment were only a few of the state's thriving industries. The unquestionable value of this development for the creation of a better life reconciled many North Carolinians to attendant dislocations and inconveniences. But it could not blind them to the sweatshop quality that was the early foundation of so much of the progress. Most North Carolinians yearned for still further industrial advance, but they also hoped for a greater diversity of industrial opportunities and a growing sensitivity on the part of the corporation toward the physical and psychological needs of the laborer.

Caldwell County has the largest known deposit of ilmenite in the world, Surry County the largest open-face granite quarry, and Vance County the nation's largest tungsten mine. In the 1950s North Carolina produced 100 percent of the nation's kaolin, 70 percent of the ground and scrap mica, and 35 percent of the feldspar.

Mount Olive Pickle Company, Mount Olive, Wayne County, was begun in 1926 and now produces over twenty million jars a year. Cucumbers (and the indispensable dill) are grown in Duplin, Sampson, Lenoir, Harnett, and Wayne counties.

42

Vendors and Lenders

Patient and Physician

The stock-market crash of 1929 foreshadowed a halt to a long period of commercial growth in North Carolina. Since the beginning of the century, urban development had generated a proliferation of wholesale enterprises as well as retail shops and stores. Banks, savings and loan associations, insurance companies, and other financial institutions multiplied in North Carolina as they did across the nation. Its publicists pointed out that the state's half-billion dollars in bank resources in 1927 represented a 200-percent increase in just one decade. Banking grew in North Carolina at a rate double the national average, and the per capita income of Tar Heels in the 1920s gained at a rate more than triple that of the country as a whole.

But figures expressed as rates of growth from very small beginnings masked North Carolina's relatively weak financial and commercial position on the eve of the crash. For example, the state's total bank resources in 1929 were barely a third of the average in other states. When farm income plummeted by two thirds between 1929 and 1933, it was not only business but the very life of the state that was threatened.

The first big bank in North Carolina to go under was Asheville's Central Bank and Trust Company, which held millions in bond-borrowed city and county money. A last-ditch attempt to stave off collapse with city funds sent the bank's president to prison, and, as hometown boy Thomas Wolfe described it in *You Can't Go Home Again*, led to the suicide of the former mayor. The eighteen Asheville bank failures of 1929 were multiplied statewide several times in the next three years and stood at 215 in March 1933. The drop in retail sales cut drastically into tax receipts and in turn into public salaries and other expenditures. Bank resources fell by a quarter and unemployment skyrocketed.

After a national bank holiday was declared in early 1933, Roosevelt's first Congress passed an Emergency Banking Act, which fostered the reopening of sound institutions. Aided by loans from the Reconstruction Finance Corporation, the creation of the Federal Deposit Insurance Corporation, and additional federal programs, most of North Carolina's financial institutions were soon stabilized. Such measures salvaged the fiscal integrity of the state, but massive injections of relief were also needed simply to ward off widespread starvation.

(Opposite) Asheville's Pack Square, ca. 1929. The new city hall is in the middle distance. The Legal Building, on the square at the right, housed the Central Bank and Trust Company. Courtesy Wright Langley.

In 1928 the Greensboro Junior League modeled fashions in the Carolina Theatre, Greensboro, Guilford County. Courtesy Carolina Theatre. Built as a movie theater and unchanged except for new seats, the theater opened with *Painting the Town* in 1927.

Another Carolina Theatre survives, built as the Durham Auditorium in 1926 by Milburn and Heister of Washington, D.C. It was adapted to show movies in 1929 and continues in that role on Roney St., Durham, Durham County.

Bar at Fayetteville packed with Fort Bragg soldiers. Robert P. Harriss Papers. World War II brought North Carolina scores of new military bases and expanded those already there, like Fort Bragg, which grew to almost a hundred thousand troops. Fayetteville gained both problems and riches from its gigantic neighbor.

Two of the most important New Deal relief programs were the Civilian Conservation Corps (CCC) and the Works Progress Administration (WPA). By late 1935 there were more than three score CCC camps in North Carolina. They provided work, wages, and board for thousands of young men engaged in flood-control and reforestation projects, road building, and the like. Reforestation of what had been worn-out cotton and tobacco land near Raleigh revived a large area that was subsequently included within Umstead State Park. CCC workers built a migratory bird refuge at Swan Quarter complete with ponds, seawalls, fire towers, and truck and foot trails. Other workers quartered in the western mountains supplied labor used in completing Mount Mitchell State Park, on the highest peak east of the Missis-

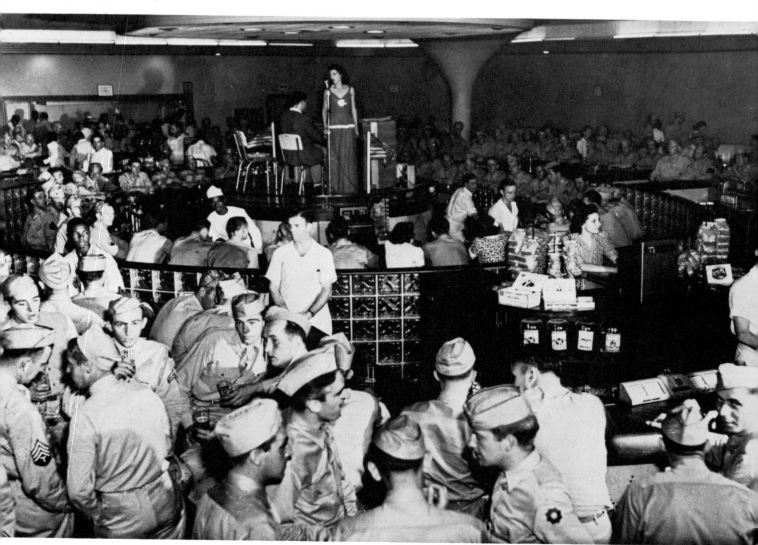

sippi. Others worked on portions of the Blue Ridge Parkway and the Great Smoky Mountains National Park.

The WPA, broader in scope and enrollment, found work for the unemployed on roads, bridges, buildings, airports, and other construction projects. But programs were also provided by the WPA for unemployed artists, writers, scholars, musicians, and actors. One group was paid to locate and record the personal narratives of former slaves, another to compile a state guidebook, still others to undertake historical research. By the time it was phased out in 1943, the WPA had spent $172,000,000 on projects employing some 225,000 Tar Heels.

Another federal relief endeavor was the planned community of Penderlea, launched in Pender County in 1934. To provide farmers living on marginal land with a fresh start (as well as to restore the land), the government bought a 4,000-acre woodland tract and built 142 houses on 20-acre homesteads. Each had a four- to six-room dwelling, barn, poultry house, hog house, smokehouse, washhouse, hot and cold running water, and electricity. A lake, school, and community center were provided, each family being allowed to buy its homestead on favorable terms. When the first phase was completed in 1936, a new one was begun with the acquisition of 6,000 more acres and the construction of 158 additional homesteads.

These and other measures stopped the economic tailspin of the early 1930s and brought about a slow recovery in the years following. By 1937 nearly all indexes of business activity—including bank deposits, life insurance sales, retail trade, construction contracts, and freight revenues—showed substantial gains. "Grinning storekeepers," reported the *Greensboro Daily News*, "told of having sold out their Christmas stock for the first time in seven years." By the fall of 1939, with the war in Europe hampering cotton and tobacco exports but otherwise boosting the Tar Heel economy, the trauma of the depression was fading. New activity at Fort Bragg and other military installations in the state further aided recovery and enabled a Durham paper early in 1941 to headline a report: "State's Business Soars to Boom-Time Peaks." Happy days were here again!

Rough Ridge Tunnel, Blue Ridge Parkway, milepost 349, McDowell County.

Although the CCC's main work was reforestation and soil and flood control, its tasks expanded to include disaster relief and the construction of facilities in state and national parks. North Carolina's legacy from the many camps located there may be seen in such structures as the stone lodge in Morrow Mountain State Park, Stanly County; the heart-pine buildings used now as campsites at Singletary Lake, Bladen County; the migratory bird refuge at Swan Quarter, Hyde County; and the stone bridges and walls along the 469 miles of the Blue Ridge Parkway.

Penderlea was not the first planned rural community in North Carolina. St. Helena, Pender County, and Castle Hayne, New Hanover County, were successfully developed early in this century by Hugh MacRae of Wilmington as agricultural colonies for immigrants.

Sweethearts and Rivals

Heavy involvement of government in business—and vice versa—began before the depression, was quickened by it, and became a permanent feature of the economic landscape in the New Deal and war years. But many an entrepreneur was convinced that his was a lonely struggle against the economic elements, in which he prospered or perished solely according to his wits. Business journals expended much ink on the evils of government regulation and the ennoblement of unfettered competition. Burlington textile baron J. Spencer Love told an Antitrust Subcommittee of the United States Senate as much in a 1955 hearing. Government, he assured the Senate, could not regulate the law of supply and demand. Then business, interposed a Wyoming senator, did not need antitrust laws. Love agreed. Neither did business need price controls, the senator continued. Love agreed again. Then, observed the legislator, business did not need government regulation in general. Love answered that business would be much better off without it. "Then you don't need a great deal of tariff protection," the senator stated. "Well, you sort of have me there," was Love's reply.

But the business ambience of the mid-twentieth century owed little to the spirit of the frontier. Like farmers, businessmen functioned within a complex network of integrated and mutually dependent private and public associations. A strong element of competition remained, adding spice and zest to the working day, but it operated within carefully coordinated matrices, such as that which linked the service station manager with an international brotherhood of oil riggers, refiners, common carriers, auto assembly workers, licensees, insurers, and the like. The character of modern business was in some respects incompatible with the traits that traditionally defined what it was to be a Tar Heel.

Business ventures blossomed or fizzled daily for all that. When Malcolm McLean of Red Springs went into the trucking business in 1934 he had one truck, which he drove himself. But a great new day was just dawning for trucking with the introduction of balloon tires,

Malcolm P. McLean. Courtesy McLean Trucking Company. A native of Maxton, Robeson County, McLean began to work in 1931 at a service station and glimpsed the possibilities of road hauling. He borrowed to buy a truck in which to haul the gasoline to his station and branched out to hauling dirt for WPA road construction and then to transporting textiles to New York. In the 1970s his company was one of the largest trucking companies in the nation.

which minimized truck damage to highways, and new engine and drive systems for power on the road. Thirty years later, McLean's firm, the fifth largest in the country, owned 5,000 trucks and trailers and 65 terminals in 20 states. McLean's Winston-Salem facility had the largest individually owned truck terminal in the world in 1954, and the rise of trucking was doing much to offset the relative weakness of North Carolina's port facilities.

A key factor in the post-depression business surge in North Carolina was the role of large urban banks. The outstanding example for many years was First Union National Bank in Charlotte. Founded in 1908, First Union made a number of important mergers in the 1950s and 1960s, notably with Cameron-Brown of Raleigh, a bond and mortgage company. First Union was the state's third largest bank in 1966, with 140 offices in 67 North Carolina communities and Nassau in the Bahamas.

Still more important to North Carolina's business was Wachovia Bank and Trust Company of Winston-Salem. Both founder-president Francis H. Fries and, following his death in 1931, his successor, Robert M. Hanes, were scions of great textile families. By an ambitious series of mergers, including that with black-owned-and-operated Forsyth Saving and Trust Company in 1930, Wachovia developed into the largest bank between Washington, D.C., and Atlanta. Its billion-and-a-half dollars in resources ranked it in 1969 as one of the major banking firms in the nation. North Carolina National Bank (NCNB), third largest in the region from the day it was chartered, was formed in 1960 by the merger of large banks in Charlotte and Greensboro in a calculated challenge to Wachovia's southeastern leadership.

The architecture of corporate finance and commerce became as much the symbol as the substance of North Carolina's incipient economic maturity. Downtown shops and retail outlets retreated toward the urban periphery as soaring professional and commercial buildings transformed city skylines. Space for horizontal expansion and construction was ample in North Carolina but lateral growth alone could not fulfill the sense of pride or the vaulting aspiration of the new corporate age. For this it would take skyscrapers, and North Carolina now boasted the financial resources to convert the new business attitudes into significant architectural statements. Major banks were leaders in setting the trend.

A symbol of another kind was the modern department store. In a sense, department store layout and architecture represented the extent to which women, in particular, were experiencing emancipation from the fetters of tradition. The elevator and escalator that carried shoppers effortlessly through capitalism's cornucopia of wares belied the slow and difficult transition of women from ancient roles, but the plenty and convenience of the department store was perhaps as much an inspiration as a reflection of social change. The stores

Courtesy McLean Trucking Company.

The Bankamericard, introduced to North Carolina by North Carolina National Bank (NCNB) in 1967, was created by the Bank of America in California. Courtesy NCNB.

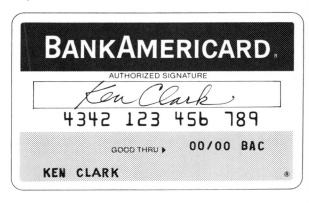

William Henry Belk Hall, built in 1955, Davidson College, Davidson, Mecklenburg County. Courtesy Davidson College. As a merchandising innovator in North Carolina, Belk borrowed many ideas from John Wanamaker of Philadelphia, also a Presbyterian philanthropist. Fixed prices, cash sales, and returnable purchases made Belk stores different and instantly successful.

North Carolina Mutual Life Insurance Company's second building (1921), now Mechanics and Farmers Bank, W. Parrish St., Durham. Courtesy North Carolina Mutual Life Insurance Company.

played an important part in generating a "revolution of rising expectations" among those who were lured from one tempting display to another in fairylands of material abundance.

Perhaps the prince of Tar Heel tradesmen of the era was William Henry Belk of Charlotte. Belk opened his first dry-goods store at Monroe in 1888 and, by the time of his death in 1952, had built a sprawling system of department stores. But the more than 400 Belk stores in 18 states and Puerto Rico in 1970 were not organized as a chain. Instead, Belk and his successors associated in partnership arrangements under which each store was operated as an independent unit, though each was supplied from Belk's warehouses in Charlotte and elsewhere. More conventionally managed but similarly successful was the Rose's Stores network of over 200 units in 9 states. Founder Paul H. Rose of Northampton County had launched his "five and dime" operation at Henderson in 1915.

It is due these titans of commerce to acknowledge that some of them became lavish philanthropists, patrons of the arts and letters, and community leaders. None could match the largesse of James B.

Rose's Stores imitated Woolworth's. Those in Warrenton (ca. 1933), Warren County, and in Littleton (1927), Halifax County, are virtually unchanged.

North Carolina Mutual and Provident Association directors, 1911. Courtesy North Carolina Mutual Life Insurance Company. Seated around the desk, from left: Dr. A. M. Moore, second president; John M. Avery, home office administrator; John Merrick, first president; Edward Merrick, treasurer; and C. C. Spaulding, general manager and third president.

Duke's Duke Endowment, but Belk, for example, established the John M. Belk Memorial Fund, through which millions in donations were made to churches, orphanages, and educational institutions, chiefly Presbyterian. Davidson College was a principal recipient of Belk gifts.

Minority-owned enterprises, laboring under added burdens, rarely attained the stature of regional significance; and the wonder is that a few did. A remarkable saga of black free enterprise is the North Carolina Mutual Life Insurance Company of Durham. The Mutual was begun in 1899 by ex-slave John Merrick, salesman C. C. Spaulding, and Dr. Aaron McD. Moore. Merrick and Moore had died by the end of 1923, but Spaulding then presided over a business that covered eleven states and the District of Columbia. At Spaulding's own death in 1952, North Carolina Mutual was a nationwide concern with almost a hundred and eighty million dollars of insurance in force, a figure that would be quadrupled by 1970. It was, in fact, the largest black-owned business in the United States.

Siren Song

The business of tourism, destined to become a major industry in North Carolina, developed haltingly in the years before World War II. Many travelers passed through the state en route to and from winter playgrounds in sunny Florida, but few were tempted, or even invited, to tarry. From the window of a speeding train or automobile the North Carolina scene was one of "rutted roads winding aimlessly off through piney woods," in the eyes of one traveler, ". . . a slab shanty, unpainted, forlorn, dismal, lop-sided; a dooryard as shaggy as a barber's Saturday night; an untended field runnelled with gulleys and grown up in sassafras sprouts; a scrub-cow, a razor-back hog, a swarm of lank dogs; a tumble-down rail fence; and everywhere the multiplying signs of slackness and untidiness and indifference."

In 1924, humorist Irvin S. Cobb felt constrained to come to North Carolina's defense. "What North Carolina should provide," he wrote, "is a beneficent hold-up man . . . who'd halt every train and . . . tell all the travelers what they were missing. His work would be in the nature of a liberal education to numbers . . . who apparently think of North Carolina only in terms of Asheville, a health resort, and Pinehurst . . . where one may break the long jump to the Florida Peninsula and . . . shoot a mess of quail or lay by a few holes of golf."

But it was still not precisely clear what there was to see or do beyond the limits of Asheville and Pinehurst. Spokesmen for the storied coast or picturesque mountains must also concede that they were accessible only to the heartiest adventurers, that tourist accommodations were uncertain at the journey's end.

Tourism as seen by a native: "I resented, and still do resent, being quaint, stimulating, and strange. It's like being background music for somebody else's Technicolor daydreams." Shackelford and Weinberg, *Our Appalachia.*

The Lost Colony, an outdoor drama, performed during the summer season, Roanoke Island, Dare County. Photograph by J. Foster Scott. Courtesy Manteo Tourist Bureau.

Fort Raleigh, Roanoke Island, Dare County, a 1950 reconstruction of Ralph Lane's earthworks of 1585, which formed the earliest English settlement on the North American continent.

Deliberate attempts to attract tourists were infrequent before the late 1940s, by which time paved roads and hotels were fairly common. A Roanoke Island commemoration of the three hundred and fiftieth anniversary of the birth of Virginia Dare, first English child born in America, was a prewar event that presaged the future drawing power of North Carolina for visitors from other sections of the country. The 1937 event featured an outdoor drama written by Pulitzer Prize-winner Paul Green of Chapel Hill and entitled *The Lost Colony*. President and Mrs. Roosevelt and critic Brooks Atkinson gave the play high marks in its first summer. Scheduled to be performed only one season, *The Lost Colony* was repeated annually until it was interrupted by the war, and since the war has become a permanent summer entertainment.

The success of *The Lost Colony* inspired similar historical dramas in later years. The most popular of these included Kermit Hunter's two mountain epics, *Unto These Hills*, which opened in 1949 at Cherokee, and *Horn in the West*, begun two years later at Boone. The rise of tourism at these extreme ends of the state helped generate funds for the restoration of Fort Raleigh at Roanoke and the

Visitors touring Council Chamber, Tryon Palace, New Bern, Craven County. Courtesy Tryon Palace Restoration.

North Carolina State Ports Authority, Wilmington, New Hanover County. Courtesy of the Authority. The facilities —ample berthing space as well as vast open and sheltered storage—make Wilmington attractive to shipping.

inauguration of mountain attractions such as "The Land of Oz" on Beech Mountain at Banner Elk, Tweetsie Railroad near Blowing Rock, and sundry others. The lure of mountain ski slopes, deep-sea fishing, wide beaches, and rhododendron-bowered trails added to the tourist influx.

Public and private campaigns were launched to advertise such attractions across the nation and abroad. The State Department of Conservation and Development's Travel and Promotion Division took a leading role in these activities, as did the Travel Council established during the Hodges administration. Private enterprise created the Innkeepers' Association in 1945, the Restaurant Association in 1947, and the Motel Association in 1954, all with the promotion of tourism as part of their rationale.

The rebuilding of the Tryon Palace at New Bern in the 1950s was a milestone in the growth of interest in historic restoration and preservation that also aided tourism. Local initiative often played the key role in such projects, which restored the eighteenth-century Moravian village of Salem and whole clusters of early buildings at Edenton, Halifax, Murfreesboro, Wilmington, and other towns. The battleship U.S.S. *North Carolina* at Wilmington, the Biltmore estate at Asheville, the Oconaluftee Indian Village, Maggie Valley Ghost Town, and numerous other ventures, often frankly commercial in conception, contributed toward North Carolina's advancing reputation as a tourist mecca. So did a plethora of parks, museums, battlegrounds, sports events, and scenic attractions.

Travelers in 1969 spent over three quarters of a billion dollars in North Carolina. Nearly half a million tourists were received that year at the state's first two "welcome centers." They came for the Highland Games, the Fiddler's Convention, the Hollering Contest, the Herring Festival, the Ramp-eating Festival, and the Man-Will-Never-Fly Memorial Society's annual meeting at Nags Head. They looked for the Brown Mountain Lights, puzzled over the Devil's Tramping Ground, waited for the Maco Ghost—and searched in vain for the after-dinner cocktail. (The quaint Tar Heel approach to mealtime alcohol was called "brown-bagging," and it remained a puzzle and nuisance to visitors until mixed drinks were legalized in most counties in the late 1970s.)

Irvin S. Cobb could rest in peace: the rush to get through North Carolina had ended.

Selling Point

By the 1950s a booming North Carolina wholesale and retail trade led the South Atlantic Region. The state had become the hub of the eastern seaboard's trucking industry, with the home offices of more long-time interstate trucking firms than any other state in the union. The wholesale trade of Charlotte exceeded that of Richmond by 55 percent and was gaining rapidly on Atlanta. There were 41,000 retail and nearly 6,000 wholesale establishments between Murphy and Manteo.

In port facilities and seagoing business, North Carolina ranked well behind Savannah and Norfolk but had overtaken the ports of South Carolina in business volume. With the aid of the State Ports Authority, established in 1945, Wilmington's maritime business rose steadily. By 1968 it was handling the cargoes of more than 500 ships, 23,000 trucks, and 8,000 railroad cars per year. Morehead City, with its shallower harbor, handled less than half of Wilmington's commerce but hoped for greater progress following completion in 1968 of a bulk facility with a half-mile-long conveyor belt and 600,000 square feet of warehouse space.

The most notable phenomenon in retail trade was a vast shift from smaller to larger places and stores. Small towns, bypassed by highways and airlines, often withered as the large urban centers sprouted shopping centers. Trade tended to shift from the downtown areas of cities to those retail centers. The intensive character of urban trade made possible many kinds of specialty shops and enterprises, from high-fashion stores to specialized medical services, that less populous areas could not hope to support. From the business perspective, as from others, the process of urbanization was the really dramatic development of the twentieth century.

Store in Cameron Village, 1950. N.C. State Archives. The largest shopping center in the Southeast when it opened in the 1950s, Cameron Village had forty stores, all on street level; underground wiring; covered sidewalks; free parking for fifteen hundred cars; and carefully regulated lighting and building codes.

"A grocery store of the early twenties was a proud specialty store, aloof from general merchandise. Gathering groceries in a cart would have been seen as the first step in shoplifting. And besides, merchandise was stacked to the ceiling in uncertain pyramids, and the practiced hand of the clerk, holding a long, hooked wand, was necessary to bring down some Gold Dust or White House Coffee or Mother's Cocoa, without bringing it all down." *The State*, March 1980.

Supermarkets evolved in California and Texas in the post-World War I era but became widespread only after World War II created shortages of time and labor and an abundance of cars and good roads. Supermarkets with the convenience of everything under one roof, unlimited free parking, and self service provided efficient and cheap marketing. They applied the department-store concept to the sale of food and household products.

Going to Town

Tobacco Towns

A statistical analyst, confronted with figures showing the importance of industry in North Carolina, in 1970 would have assumed that, like all other leading industrial states, most of its people lived in cities. Surprisingly, however, this was not the case; alone among such states North Carolina remained more rural and small-town than urban, though nearly two-thirds of all Americans lived in cities in 1970.

The reasons were well enough known. Early North Carolina, burdened by shallow harbors and ports, its terrain laced with rivers and swamps that deterred road building, came late to the process of urbanization. Only when the center of population shifted in the nineteenth century to the Piedmont was the rise of cities possible, and other factors made for slow growth even then. One such factor was the nature of the state's leading industry: textiles. Because small textile plants were as efficient as large ones, textile manufacturers were not tempted to cling to the largest urban centers. Rather, textile and apparel firms found it desirable to remain in small-town or rural settings where wage scales were lowest. Thus North Carolina's small towns held on more tenaciously—and its cities grew more slowly—than in most of the country.

It was not until the 1880s that as much as 5 percent of the Tar Heel population lived in urban areas; and not until 1940 could North Carolina claim its first city of more than a hundred thousand people: Charlotte. There were six such metropolitan areas in North Carolina in 1970, but none was comparable to major non-North Carolina cities in its degree of urban concentration. No city dominated the life of the state, but five of the leading six in 1970 lay in an arc along the route of the Southern Railway, developed in the mid-nineteenth century to link Raleigh, Durham, Greensboro, and Winston-Salem to Charlotte.

The Coastal Plain, its broken topography still not knitted by compensatory highways and railroads, developed no sizable urban area even by North Carolina standards. Wilmington, with less than fifty thousand inhabitants, was the largest place east of Raleigh but still somewhat isolated from the rest of the state. More representative of the very gradual urbanizing process in the east was a cluster of towns in the central Coastal Plain: Rocky Mount, Wilson, Greenville, Goldsboro, and Kinston.

(Opposite) Tobacco market, Wilson, Wilson County. North Carolina Collection. Until recently, Wilson was the leading bright leaf tobacco market in the world with a score of warehouses, of which Smith's was the largest. Over four hundred lots of tobacco can be auctioned each hour as the auctioneer and buyers move down the rows conducting the bidding in seemingly unintelligible chants and almost imperceptible signals.

Until 1915 tobacco was piled on the market floor to be sold; since then it has been placed in shallow, oak split baskets, almost all of which are made in Yadkin County. In the oldest plant now in operation, the Yadkin Basket Company, Shacktown community, Yadkinville, ten men make three hundred baskets a day. In the whole county, sixty-five men make almost half a million baskets a year.

The first bale of Dacron leaving the DuPont Kinston plant (N.C. #11, east of Kinston) in 1953. Courtesy DuPont de Nemours and Company, Inc. DuPont was the developer of this polyester staple used in durable and wrinkle-free fabrics. An industrial grade is made for fire hose, tires, and other products where strength is vital.

The five towns ranged in population from Kinston (22,000) to Rocky Mount (34,000), with only Greenville undergoing any significant increase in the 1960s. Kinston and Goldsboro actually declined during the decade. In 1860 all but Rocky Mount had been among the ten largest towns in the state; in 1970 none was. Such prosperity as they enjoyed could be attributed largely to the fact that they were the five largest bright leaf tobacco markets in the world, with Wilson the world leader.

"Marketing," as Jonathan Daniels wrote of these towns in 1941, "is the farmer's fate but the towns' frenzy. . . . It is a competition for the tobacco between the towns which exceeds even the wildest moments in the Coastal Plain baseball league. On all highways are huge billboards advising the farmer to sell his tobacco in the Such-andsuch tobacco market which always gives a fair deal and high prices. . . . Whole communities [are] united in the will to make the farmer happy within their gates. It was not accident that Kinston . . . kept for so many years . . . the gay and good-looking girls in its gaudy Sugar Hill. . . . Loving the farmer is the chief industry from Raleigh to the sea."

Kinston labored forlornly through the depression, when every industry but the Hines Brothers Lumber Company closed down. No Prince Charming came to kiss it into prosperity. The meat-packing plant built in 1945 and later taken over by Frosty Morn helped—but not enough. In 1953 a prince seemed actually to appear in the form of DuPont's (and the world's) first Dacron plant, "a dream come true," in the ecstatic view of the Kinston *Free Press*, "the beginnings of a new industrial era."

Perhaps so, but not for Kinston. DuPont put two thousand people to work and by 1962 had pumped fourteen million dollars into the local economy and lent impetus to the opening of an industrial education center (which later evolved into Lenoir Community College). Nevertheless, the population of Kinston, after expanding for a time, decreased by 10 percent during the 1960s, tarnishing the luster of the "new industrial era." Real growth was not even foreseeable; what Kinston could realistically count on was mere survival on the strength of its tobacco, Dacron, and shirt factories; its lumber mills and its food processors.

It was much the same in Rocky Mount, which, though it was not faced with imminent decline, was not growing much either. What visitors remembered most about Rocky Mount was not its scattering of cotton-yarn and lumber mills, its producers of cottonseed oil, cordage, overalls, and the like, or even the spring fling known as the Gallopade—but rather the June German. This was a ball held annually since the 1880s and always in a gaily decorated tobacco warehouse. A Methodist pastor in 1923 worked himself into a froth over "women under the influence of liquor . . . bottles dropped on the

Couples waiting for the music to begin at a June German, Rocky Mount, Edgecombe County. Courtesy *Tar Heel* magazine, Killebrew Studio.

Dancing was a common recreation for everyone in the 1930s, '40s, and '50s. Photograph by Hal Rericha. N.C. State Archives. Robert Simpson describes the era: "When I was in high school, what was the thing was bobby socks an' slicked-back hairdos an' bebop music, all this kinda stuff. Doin' the shag. Even the music was real simple, a straight direct beat. You could dance fast an' then you'd do the slow ones, and it wasn't supercool, it was romantic. Maybe we didn't know how lucky we were." Wolcott, *Rose Hill.*

ballroom floor" and other, enormities of the revelers. But this was in the years when the punch was sometimes spiked with as much as forty gallons of "bootleg," and the illicit hooch was half the fun. Jonathan Daniels, who witnessed a more sedate affair in 1941, thought it still "the biggest dance in the State, maybe in America—probably the world." German weekend meant thousands of dancers and onlookers and a ball that began at 9:00 P.M. and ended at dawn when "everyone would pile into cars and head for the beach." It was always a big-band affair, too, with the likes of Jimmy Dorsey or hometown boy Kay Kyser. But interest dwindled in the 1960s when other recreational opportunities crowded it out, and the German slid quietly into oblivion.

The tobacco towns that fared best were those that had something extra going for them besides the leaf and some small industrial concerns. The ability of Goldsboro, for example, to maintain a faltering pace owed much to the federal government. The establishment of Seymour Johnson Air Base there during World War II gave the area a major military installation and a vital injection to local payrolls. Goldsboro's retail trade held up well because the town had commercial primacy over large portions of several surrounding counties; and there were also locally made leather products, electronic components, machinery—there was even an easternmost outpost of the furniture industry. But not even the Strategic Air Command could safeguard Goldsboro against the uncertainties of the postwar epoch, and the town could not keep pace with similar communities to the west.

The slight, relative advantage at Wilson was mainly Atlantic Christian College (operated by the Christian Church), Hackney Body Works, and two million square feet of tobacco warehouse space (including Smith's, the world's largest tobacco auction market). Wilson's annual tobacco festival and exposition paid due homage to the "folk dance attended by chanting," as Daniels termed it, which marked every market day between mid-August and Thanksgiving and poured green bills into the local economy. Processions of buyers during these days moved quickly between rows piled high with tobacco, while clusters of farmers trailed along to hear the bids and reject or register those made on their own baskets. What astonished the neophyte was the ability of all those people to make sense of the auctioneer's jet-propelled "bafflegab" of numbers and exhortations, but somehow the procession rolled on and the leaf was sold. The Wilson and Greenville markets each handled over seventy million pounds a year.

Greenville faced much the same economic strains of fluctuating markets and black and white exodus as the other towns but weathered them better because of the expansion of its college. East Carolina Teachers College ("Eeseeteesee," as it was known down east), originally a girls' school, was long an ugly duckling in North Carolina's extensive system of higher education. A period of aggressive leadership after World War II carried it rapidly to higher status as East Carolina College and, ultimately, University, complete with medical school and big-time athletics. Greenville was also blessed with a respectable mixture of business and industry, including plastics, concrete products, cotton yarn, lumber, fertilizer, bricks, metalworks, and meat-packing. By 1970 the town could claim educational and cultural leadership over a large section of eastern North Carolina.

But nowhere in eastern North Carolina was the future particularly promising. "[O]nce a year," as Jonathan Daniels concluded, "while the auctioneer chants and sways and the buyers march to his chanting, the intoxication of riches spreads through the towns and overflows the land. That exaltation is emphasized by the sadder years when the chant is a wail and merchants and bankers and farmers walk together in sorrow."

East Hargett

The passage of Jim Crow laws and the practice of racial discrimination after about 1890 created in most North Carolina towns and cities clear patterns of racial separation. Those black houses and businesses that had emerged in earlier years within white-majority districts were pushed out, often leaving blacks as the sole occupants of designated fringes or islands within the urban area. Placement in such areas of segregated schools and other public and private facilities that served only black patrons minimized contact between the races and suspended for generations the attainment of the economic and social aspirations of the black communities.

This pattern was clear enough in Raleigh, the state capital, though perhaps less rigidly imposed than in most urban areas of the South. Various factors, not always discriminatory, combined in the first decades of the twentieth century to concentrate black business along a stretch of Raleigh's East Hargett Street, which became, in effect, the city's "Negro Main Street." The acquisition of real estate there by black commission merchant Berry O'Kelly and the erection in 1915 of the Lightner Building for professional offices helped make East Hargett Street attractive to black businesses. By 1923 blacks outnumbered whites there, and, though the black influx leveled off with the coming of the depression, East Hargett remained predominantly black through the 1960s.

East Hargett Street early gained a good reputation in the city. Distinctly middle-class, it drew black doctors, lawyers, tailors, beauticians, dentists, and barbers, as well as black insurance companies, undertakers, a black theater, hotel, bank, and a wide assortment of retail stores. But the street was at least as important socially as it was economically. The annual black Debutante Ball originated there, and the hotel dining room, in the recollection of an old-timer, "used to be on the front and everybody ate in there. That was THE place to go to eat. You could go in and get a soft drink or coffee or the like and a piece of pie and sit and talk half the day if you wanted to." Many people, according to another, "just came and stood outside and looked in; they could see all the important people there."

The poolroom on East Hargett was the gathering place for a clientele less elite than that at the hotel dining room. "Fellows who had hot stuff to sell," said a denizen, "would show up at the poolroom because that's where the folks were. Since the poolroom has been off the street, got burned in '56, there's no place to hang out." The American Legion clubroom over the Royal Theater was another popular East Hargett social resort.

East Hargett flourished because it was convenient to the heavily black southeastern section of Raleigh and to other scattered black neighborhoods. Also it lay hard by the city's central downtown business streets and had a share of white patronage. Black clients knew that their accounts were welcome there and that the street's restrooms and drinking fountains carried no "white only" signs. But the popularity of the street owed something in the 1920s and 1930s to the convivial informality that pervaded it. "Anyone who wanted to pass the time away and just generally 'shoot the breeze' made his way to Hargett St.," said one veteran. "There was no YMCA then . . . the churches had no activities to interest young men, and the

Berry O'Kelly (1860–1931). N.C. State Archives. O'Kelly began as a small merchant in the black community of Method, now part of Raleigh. His efforts on behalf of better agriculture, education, and industry led to a variety of tasks: chairman of a local school committee that consolidated three rural black schools into the Berry O'Kelly Training School; founder of the National Negro Business League; president of realty and shoe companies; chairman of a life insurance company; and vice-president of the Raleigh branch of the Mechanics and Farmers Bank of Durham.

59

Roger O'Kelly (1880–1962). Yale University Alumni Records. Roger O'Kelly explained how he managed: "My almost sole dependence now, when not conversing with deaf-mutes, is pencil and pad: they carried me through Shaw and Yale and they have carried me through many important business deals. One can write with much more care and deliberation than he can speak. Did you ever think of it? a pencil puts one on his guard. Spoken words are easily forgotten, written words stay and are remembered." *The Silent Worker*, March 1927.

Wonderland Theatre, Durham. Duke University Manuscript Department. This 1920 theater once stood on the main street of Hayti, a black community in Durham. It was used by tobacco workers in 1934 to hold union meetings, which resulted in the formation of two Tobacco Workers International Union locals.

city had none. . . . It was the only place Negroes could go for ice cream even. . . . [O]ne group hung out on the south side of the street and another group on the north side. The north side group was made up of professional men who had offices on the street. . . . The younger group hung around on the south side of the street. If you were looking for fun, hilarity, talking about girls, whistling at girls, etc., then you joined the young group on the south side."

The Raleigh black community's most charismatic personalities were to be found on the street as well as its most talented pro-

Young Men's Institute (no longer used), Asheville, Buncombe County. Founded by George Vanderbilt for the black community and the construction workers at Biltmore, the YMI, built 1892–93, housed shops as well as residence and meeting rooms and served as a center of black education and religion in the city.

fessional men and entrepreneurs. Roger Demosthenes O'Kelly, America's only deaf-mute lawyer, a graduate of Yale Law School, established an office there in 1921. He was a widely respected expert on real estate transactions, domestic relations, and corporate law, and he served white clients as well as black.

East Hargett was where the rural poor came in wagons on Saturdays to sell their eggs and butter and visit the rummage sales (or, when these were banned, the secondhand clothing and furniture stores). It was where the Negro newspaper was published, where the professional and social clubs met and had their chief functions. The Raleigh Safety Club, a cooperative funeral society, met there for years on the upper floor of the Odd Fellows Building. It paid a dollar per member to the family of any member at the time of his death. A ladies' auxiliary also provided food and other assistance to the bereaved.

The 1940s brought changes in the character of East Hargett, but the street continued to be the focus of black business in the Raleigh area. Traffic and parking congestion drove some of the doctors, undertakers, and other professionals elsewhere in quest of more space. Many businesses previously owned by one individual became partnerships or corporations, while a general improvement in the civil position of blacks made them less dependent upon black-owned businesses. Gradually, East Hargett Street became more impersonal in its business style, less important in its social dimension. But the street in its heyday provided the black community with services and opportunities that were available through no other channel.

"Every Saturday the people from all these towns, black and white, would pour into Raleigh on the blue-black roads that Governor Kerr Scott had built for them, and they would all go to Montgomery Ward's and Briggs' Hardware to spend their money quickly and then, while the women were looking at dresses in Hudson-Belk's, the men would lounge around in the public squares, the whites in their square and the blacks in theirs, all of them very unselfconscious in their faded blue overalls. There was some drinking, whiskey in the white square and Catawba grape in the black one, and by eight or nine o'clock on Saturday night the emergency rooms would be full of the victims of stabbing and shooting wounds." "Going Home to Raleigh," *Harper's Magazine*, April 1970.

Pauli Murray, 1977. Photograph by Jim
Sparks. Courtesy Durham Herald Company. The law school of the University
of North Carolina rejected Pauli Murray
on racial grounds; ironically, the university had inherited land and money from
her white ancestors.

Following is a description of a black
laborer's house in Durham in the 1920s:
"One enters a bare room lit by an open
electric bulb! The chief piece of furniture
is the white enamel iron double bed covered by a neat counterpane. On the left
is a golden oak bureau . . . covered with
an assortment of old medicine bottles.
On the other side is an old-fashioned
board trunk. In the center of the room,
gathered around the cast iron stove, are
grouped the family . . . seated on
straight chairs. . . . On the mantle with
the alarm clock is a vase with crepe
paper roses. Brightly colored calendars
are on the walls. . . . There are no rugs,
and not even curtains at the windows."
Brinton, "Negro in Durham."

Dukedom

A godchild of the Piedmont's Victorian-era industrial surge, the city
of Durham struggled indignantly in the middle decades of the twentieth century against its reputation as an overgrown factory town, ill
at ease with the university brought in for cultural uplift by the city's
new rich. It was more than Durham's humble beginnings and hard-
driving growth that inspired a mixture of derision and envy in others.
Durham was the raw embodiment of the persisting gulfs in the industrial New South between rich and poor, slum and suburb, squalor
and gentility.

It was no wonder that novelist Thomas Wolfe, scarred already
by the crassness that commerce had brought to his childhood home
and hamlet of Asheville, would find Durham a "dreary tobacco town"
with "a thinning squalor of cheap houses." To Wolfe and fellow under-
graduates at Chapel Hill, Durham existed to serve one need only.
Portrayed as the town of "Exeter" in *Look Homeward, Angel*, the
town was seen as a "sordid little road, unpaved, littered on both
sides with negro shacks and the dwellings of poor whites" that led to
a much-frequented brothel.

Pauli Murray, black attorney and one of the first women ordained
as an Episcopal priest, grew up in Durham in the 1920s and afterward
recalled its poorest sections in images entirely compatible with those
of Wolfe. It was a collection, she wrote, of shanty-hamlets called
"Bottoms" that clung precariously "to the banks of streams or sat
crazily on washed-out gullies and were held together by cowpaths or
rutted wagon tracks. . . . It was as if the town had swallowed more
than it could hold and had regurgitated, for the Bottom was an odious
conglomeration of trash piles, garbage dumps, cow-stalls, pigpens,
and crowded humanity. You could tell it at night by the straggling
lights from oil lamps glimmering along the hollows and the smell of
putrefaction, pig swill, cow dung, and frying food. Even if you lived
on a hill just above the Bottoms, it seemed lower and danker than the
meanest hut on a graded street."

Of graded streets there were but few in the 1920s, especially
in the Durham neighborhood of Hayti (Hay-tie). Hayti flourished in
the years of Prohibition with bootleg whiskey. Illicit liquor stores—
known and notorious as "blind tigers"—abounded and asked patrons
neither color nor creed. A den of iniquity to its detractors, Hayti was
a home place for thousands. Small black groceries and businesses
served customers by day, and some of the South's legendary blues
and jazz musicians—including "Sonny" Terry and "Blind Boy" Fuller
—brought their magic to the nights.

Elsewhere in town, for whites, there were two silent-movie
houses and a burlesque theatre. For highbrow entertainment, the
Academy of Music offered concerts and road shows. Nonetheless to

Duke University Chapel under construction in 1931. Duke University Archives.

Jonathan Daniels—ancient Raleigh antagonist of the Duke family—Durham in 1941 was still mainly muck and dilapidation. "Ragged children played in the dirt before the dirty houses," and "unpaved streets" ran "up and down hilly, muddy lanes to slums."

Needless to say, perhaps, there were more Durhams than those described by Thomas Wolfe, Pauli Murray, and Jonathan Daniels. Quite apart from attractive residential areas, an imposing tower by this time rose impressively above the Gothic and Georgian buildings of "Buck" Duke's "instant university" of the 1920s. By an enormous outlay of cash, buttressed by a forty-million-dollar endowment, Duke had transformed a small Methodist school called Trinity into a leading educational institution. By the time the foundations of its huge English chapel were laid in 1930, Duke University was a complex of

stone structures surrounding a large court. Besides its sprawling medical complex, its law school, comprehensive library, and formal gardens, Duke by the mid-1930s could even boast a powerhouse of a football team. The "Blue Devils" hosted the 1942 Rose Bowl, losing by 20 to 16 to Oregon State.

But Durham, in the 1920s, was more than its university. North Carolina College (later North Carolina Central University) had outlived its critics and was emerging as one of the South's foremost institutions of higher learning for blacks. Durham's downtown, with its twenty-odd restaurants packed into a five-block area, lacked aesthetic appeal, but the gleaming Washington Duke Hotel and the new Union Bus Terminal might well divert the eyes of the itinerant from much that was not pleasing. Every fifth American cigarette was made in the aromatic factory district, and Durham was then North Carolina's second largest city.

Efforts by owners and workers alike improved Durham's working class. West Durham, under the enlightened paternalism of mill magnate William A. Erwin, was a mill village of advanced design. Even before 1920 Erwin introduced lights and plumbing, a day-care center and playgrounds. In 1922 he built a three-story auditorium with a bowling alley, library, and classrooms for instruction in the "domestic sciences." Erwin Mills also sponsored contests and awarded prizes to those workers with the best-kept yards, or to the best in cooking and canning foods.

By the 1970s promoters could declare with only a hint of hyperbole that Main Street "meanders between sentinels of trees and potted plantings from the new County Judicial Building to the Muirhead Plaza Fountains at Five Points." Gone were most of the eateries of yesteryear; in their place was a complex of government and institutional edifices. A nationally recognized black bourgeoisie, its center of gravity located in the stunning twelve-story headquarters of the North Carolina Mutual Life Insurance Company, testified to the achievement of Durham blacks despite the "Bottoms" and other barriers to racial achievement. A Durham Symphony Orchestra gave tone to the city's cultural life, a Street-Arts Celebration drew annually fifty thousand and more people to the city's center for sociability and good cheer. A healthy rivalry pitted Durham against Raleigh and Chapel Hill for the right to house and trade with the gilded salariat of the Research Triangle.

"Altamont"

If it was ever really true that "you can't go home again," Thomas Wolfe was as good a living example of that aphorism as most. Ashevillians read his *Look Homeward, Angel* in 1929 and saw it as a mean little hatchet job, a needless reminder of the town's old grudges and past sins and grubby secrets that every town has but tries to hide. The mill hands at Durham might not flinch at Wolfe's strictures against them, but the residents of Asheville were accustomed to the image of their town as presented in travel brochures that alluringly portrayed the beauties of the "Land of the Sky." The public library would not put the book on its shelves, and the local papers gave it

Thomas Wolfe's "Old Kentucky Home," ca. 1937, Asheville, Buncombe County. N.C. State Archives.

Asheville High School, Buncombe County, built in 1927 of pink and gray granite banded with orange brick and terra cotta, is a typical product of Asheville's favorite architect, Douglas Ellington, as are the city hall and the First Baptist Church.

bad reviews. Wolfe paid his hometown one more brief visit in 1937 when his fame lent an air of glamour even to his taunts, but he probably never came back in spirit.

And, anyway, Tom had this way of needling what he loved best. He had a soft spot in his heart for the "Old Kentucky Home" ("Dixieland" in the book), his family's boardinghouse at 48 Spruce Street, but he wrote of it as a "big, cheaply constructed frame house of rambling, unplanned, gabular appearance." He spent many happy hours around Pack Square, the business center where his father's monument shop stood, but the book called the locale a "treeless brick jungle of business—cheap, ragged and ugly, and beyond all this, in indefinite patches, the houses where all the people lived, with little bright raw ulcers of suburbs further off, and the healing and concealing grace of tall massed trees." Such was "Altamont," as Asheville was called in Wolfe's novel.

Asheville during Wolfe's adolescence—the World War I era—was a place of horses and wagons and trolley cars, a saucer-like depression on the French Broad and Swannanoa rivers, overshadowed by Summit and Beaucatcher mountains. It was essentially a resort town that blossomed with color and activity from June to September and then shriveled to half its summertime size in fall and winter. For a brief period in the mid-1920s, Asheville went through a wild spell of land speculation when con men fresh from the Florida boom (and bust) moved in and pushed prices for prime lots to several thousand dollars and more a front foot. The opening of the Battery Park and George Vanderbilt Hotels in 1924 signaled a dizzy spree of building schools, parks and golf courses, a city hall and library, a tunnel through Beaucatcher Mountain, and a subdivision platted from surrounding farms.

The bubble burst, of course, in the spring of 1926 and ultimately shut down six local banks. Like a terrible omen, Wolfe's novel presaged the coming of even worse: the Great Depression, during which construction dwindled, factories closed, and even the tourist business dried up. The Edisons and Firestones and Fords still came sometimes to the Grove Park Inn during the 1930s (President Roosevelt overnighted there in 1936), but lesser mortals stayed home and the town suffered. Jonathan Daniels in 1941 found Asheville "circled with such magnificent mountains and . . . so steeply tawdry within," with a "driving, hungry, resort-town frenzy which stripped all the prettiness, all the dignity, off the town."

But Daniels was cursing the town and, indirectly, himself for not having appreciated Wolfe's genius or respected his viewpoint in the beginning. Asheville had, perhaps, a rather shabby and unkempt appearance after a decade of depression, but it nevertheless offered many advantages that the casual visitor might not notice. It was the marketing center for burley tobacco, livestock, fruits, and other farm products of western North Carolina. There was Biltmore, the striking two-hundred-fifty-room mansion of George W. Vanderbilt; a spectacular June Rhododendron Festival; a July Mountain Folk Music and Dance Festival; and various golf and tennis tournaments.

In spite of its potential, Asheville languished through the 1940s and 1950s. The quaint but unfrequented town suffered from a relative inaccessibility and the failure of local business leaders to anticipate fully the burgeoning postwar tourist boom. Emigration reduced Buncombe County's population by ten thousand during the dreary decade before 1960. But the trend was reversed in the 1960s after urban renewal projects had freshened up the town's appearance and attracted new tourist accommodations. Moreover, new highways were opened

Native Ashevillians distrusted the newcomers: ". . . it took quite a bit of education to cause the local people to accept tourists. This was one of the most provincial areas that you can imagine. They resented these Northerners coming in here: they were strange people, they didn't speak like they spoke, and they didn't dress like they dressed." Shackelford and Weinberg, *Our Appalachia.*

The Grove Park Inn, Asheville, Buncombe County, shows E. W. Grove's grandiose ideas. Built by four hundred Negro workmen brought from Atlanta and Charleston who labored round the clock, at night under klieg lights, and by tile masons from Italy, who laid every floor with handmade porcelain tile, the mammoth hotel is constructed of granite boulders hoisted into place with only chains to help.

The New Arcade, 1926, in the Federal Building, Asheville, was another of Grove's creations. Arcades are the ancestors of today's shopping malls. Latta Arcade, 1914, Charlotte, and Irvin Arcade, ca. 1930, Greensboro, are other extant examples.

Battery Park Hotel, also built by Grove and still standing but derelict, reflects the boom and bust of Asheville's 1920s.

Pisgah View Ranch Dancers, 1975. Courtesy Asheville Chamber of Commerce. These dancers from Hominy Valley are participating in the oldest folk festival in the nation, the Asheville Mountain Dance and Folk Festival, held the first week in August.

Biltmore House, Asheville, Buncombe County, 1895, designed by Richard M. Hunt, reproduces European splendor in a superlative American setting. Courtesy Biltmore House and Gardens.

through the town's mountain environs, and modern hotels replaced some of the antiquated inns and boardinghouses of the predepression boomlet.

By 1970 Asheville was alive and well again, the seventh largest city in the state, with fifty-eight thousand inhabitants. Nearly encircled by a million acres of national forest and serving as the gateway to the Great Smoky Mountains National Park, Asheville gained a year-round clientele as ski slopes opened in the adjacent hills. Year-round occupancy was also enhanced by the evolution of little Asheville Normal and Teachers College into the University of North Carolina at Asheville. By 1970 prosperity had banished the old resentment of Thomas Wolfe, and the town had learned to bestow due homage upon its prodigal son.

Colossalopolis

Demographers and urban planners looking toward the twenty-first century foresaw huge supercities stretching north and south from Los Angeles on the Pacific coast and from Boston southward to the Potomac in the East. From the perspective of 1970, North Carolina seemed unlikely in the foreseeable future to become engulfed in any such urban sprawl, but the state's leading population centers were, indeed, beginning discernibly to merge. This raised the prospect of a vast, uninterrupted urban complex, a "Charleigh" or "Ralotte" that would pave the tobacco fields of the Piedmont and make parks of its rolling forests.

The term "Triangle" was already frequently heard for the Raleigh-Durham-Chapel Hill area, though distinct rural expanses still largely separated the three. "Triad" would soon be coined to designate the Greensboro–Winston-Salem–High Point area, and a contest in the Charlotte vicinity in 1968 had brought forth the term "Metrolina" as the label for the urbanized region of which Charlotte was the hub. Moreover, all three of these incipient supercities formed points along a three-hundred-mile strip reaching from Lynchburg, Virginia, to Anderson, South Carolina, that seemed likely to become a southern version of megalopolis—with five million inhabitants—by the year 2000.

Metrolina embraced everything within a fifty-mile radius of Charlotte. It included Rock Hill, South Carolina; Hickory; Salisbury; Shelby; Monroe; and other towns and cities regarded as being in some degree related—by proximity to Charlotte or to one another. Planners deemed it useful to think in terms of such urban systems as a means of coordinating various services and activities. The time had come, they declared, when municipalities could no longer "work in a vacuum of narrow local interests."

Jefferson Standard Building, built
in 1923, Greensboro, Guilford County.
Photograph by Joann Sieburg-Baker.
N.C. State Archives.

North Carolinians, like all Americans,
endured a nightmare in the form of
summer polio epidemics that terrorized
the state from 1929 to 1948. No section
was spared these seasonal visitations.
In 1948 North Carolina had the worst
epidemic in the country with over
twenty-five hundred cases and a hundred
deaths from the disease. Apart from the
toll in human suffering, the epidemics
frequently meant disruption of school
schedules, recreational activities, and
other normal patterns of living. In 1944
Hickory, Catawba County, and in 1948
Greensboro, Guilford County, were
forced to provide special polio hospitals
to handle the numbers of cases. Only
with the introduction of the Salk vaccine
in the late 1950s was the disease finally
brought under control.

Megalopolis, then, was the urban counterpart of the central
theme of the epoch. It embodied the same sort of thinking that
impressed itself in these years on the farmer who joined a co-op, the
industrialist and businessman who learned the lessons of commercial
and industrial integration. Planning, for the urbanologist, was needed
not only to ensure a better quality of city life but also to prevent the
horrendous consequences that dogged the tracks of city growth. The

Soviet Union pursued its program of development through forced "five-year plans" and the like, but in the West it still seemed possible to realize humanity's hopes through cooperation and voluntary means. The phantom of prospective force haunted the planner's work, but the need for cooperative effort seemed evermore inescapable as the century progressed.

Metrolina in the 1960s had an aggregate population of over a million, fourth in the Southeast behind the Miami, Atlanta, and Tampa-St. Petersburg urban complexes. Its growth during the decade far outstripped that of the state (although an unequal pattern of distribution left Metrolina's southeastern corner, Union County, still heavily rural). A quarter of Metrolina's inhabitants were engaged in manufacturing—mostly in textiles and apparel, but also in furniture, non-electrical machinery, chemicals, and other products. But their manufacturing wages were lower than the state's as a whole, pulled down by the textile and apparel factories that dotted the area.

The Metrolinian tended to be slightly better educated than the typical Tar Heel (ninth-grade average), though well below the national norm. They were still mostly Democratic, but Republican candidates made big gains in the region during the 1950s and 1960s. A graduate of the area's high schools could choose from among four technical institutions, seven two-year colleges, and thirteen senior colleges without leaving Metrolina. Cultural uplift was available through the Mint Museum of Art, the Mint Museum Dance Guild, the Charlotte Symphony Orchestra, the Charlotte Opera Association, and a wide variety of satellite programs and institutions. Carowinds amusement park had lately brought popular entertainment to Metrolina on a grand scale.

Urban planners puzzled over the contradiction inherent in the evolution of Metrolina and similar supercities. Vast numbers of people identified the good life with easy access to the amenities of big-city living, but most also felt that the good life meant abundant space between oneself and one's neighbors. The effort to reconcile these ideals underlay the city's evolution into an urban region and the fostering of regional, as opposed to local, attitudes and allegiances. Hence, Metrolina was already part of a regional coordinating committee, an environmental concern association, an air quality control program, a soil and water conservation effort, an area development association, and other regional planning groups. Would Charlotte, Winston-Salem, Raleigh, and Greensboro soon be boroughs within a megalopolis? In some respects, they already were.

Leo Driehuys conducting the Charlotte Symphony Orchestra. Photograph by Art Gentile. Courtesy Charlotte Symphony Orchestra.

Express Lanes

Getting There

The provincialism that was said to be a primary trait of the quint-essential Tar Heel reflected North Carolina's geography and early pattern of growth. A want of good harbors reduced North Carolina's contact with the outside world; a superfluity of rivers and streams inhibited rather than facilitated contact among settlers. Tar Heels were slow to be drawn into either the federal Union or the Confederacy in part because it was difficult for propagandists to reach and influence them.

The sectionalism of the Carolinian arose from the peculiarity of eighteenth-century immigration into the Piedmont and Mountain sections. The settlers there did not, in the main, come from the older English and Scottish settlements in the East but rather from Germany and Ireland by way of the northern colonies. This heightened the differences between easterner and westerner and made for political ramifications that lasted well into the twentieth century.

To the extent that geographical isolation was the root of provincialism and sectionalism in North Carolina, good roads, railways, bridges, and airports were important modifiers of the traditional character traits. But facilities of modern transport and communication sufficient to alter the Tar Heel personality did not come until the twentieth century was well advanced and did not have a remarkably rapid or pronounced effect even then. By this time it was recognized that a sectionalism that expressed itself in healthy rivalry was not to be despised; a provincialism that gave to Tar Heel literature a strong sense of place was regarded as a decided asset. Well before 1970 heralds of North Carolina's movement into the mainstream of American life were reflecting soberly that this provincialism was not an unmixed blessing. As with immigrant Greeks and Chinese, more and more Tar Heels sought ways to experience the benefits of the mainstream without losing their identity in its faceless currents.

An important step toward ending North Carolina's relative isolation was taken in 1921 when the state legislature approved a $50 million bond issue—the state's largest to that date. The object of the new program, financed by automobile and gasoline taxes, was to complete and maintain a 5,500-mile system of primary roads. When finished, it would connect all of North Carolina's 100 county seats, its principal towns and cities, its state parks and state institutions, and link these with the highway systems of neighboring states. A key

Footbridge, Joyce Kilmer Memorial Forest, Nantahala National Forest, Graham County. In remote mountain valleys, bridges like this were once the only lifelines between isolated homesteads.

The 1921 Highway Act, which brought North Carolina out of the mud, was the achievement of Harriet Berry (1877–1940) through the North Carolina Good Roads Association. She campaigned in every county, organized petitions, wrote letters and circulars, and obtained money and members for the organization. Politically astute, she led the group to accomplish its aims: ambitious road legislation and a strong highway commission.

Good roads made possible the consolidation of rural schools and the use of school buses. Thomas Built Buses, Inc., High Point, Guilford County, the largest manufacturer of school buses in the world, supplies the buses. Originally a trolley manufacturer, Thomas made the New Orleans trolleys, still in use. A Thomas trolley may be seen in the High Point Museum.

73

Raleigh–Greensboro bus. N.C. State Archives.

part of the program was a central route—now Highway 70—reaching from Beaufort on the coast through Raleigh, Greensboro, and Asheville to the Tennessee line.

Besides realizing the aims of the program, the 1920s witnessed the commitment of another $50 million to the enlargement of the primary system. But money was scarce and further progress slow during most of the 1930s and 1940s. By 1948 the state had responsibility for a total of 64,000 miles of road and highways, but many secondary routes were impassable in bad weather. World War II traffic had been hard on the primary roads, and municipalities, unaided by the state, were struggling to cope with the onrushing increase in automobile traffic and the flight to suburbia. Only 7,000 miles of North Carolina's roads had any sort of hard surface.

Kerr Scott made roads a central campaign issue when he ran for governor in 1948. He promised to improve the routes used by the state's 6,000 public-school buses and to "get the farmer out of the mud." After winning election, Scott startled many by gaining legislative and referendum approval for a whopping $200 million road-bond issue. In addition to building 14,000 miles of roads, his administration oversaw the passage of the "Powell bill," which provided funds for municipal streets. This bill also helped soften the resentment of city folks over the cost to them of Scott's rural bonds.

With the federal government's entry into interstate road building in the 1950s and Governor Dan Moore's successful 1965 campaign to obtain approval of a $300 million bond issue, North Carolina emerged from its isolation and began shaking off its provincialism. In the Coastal Plain, the $10 million Wilmington Memorial Bridge was completed across the Cape Fear River in 1969. Meanwhile, the picturesque Herbert Bonner Bridge had been built over Oregon Inlet on the Outer Banks and the big Lindsay C. Warren Bridge across the

74

Hatteras Ferry. Photograph by
H. L. Powell. N.C. Department of
Transportation.

Alligator River in Tyrrell County. In the west, the most impressive
new span was that over the Green River Gorge in Polk County,
opened in 1968. Altogether, there were some 15,000 bridges in the
state system.

In places where bridges had not been built, as between Ocracoke and Cedar islands, across Currituck Sound, and over Hatteras
Inlet, the state established ferry service. The state's fleet of sixteen
ferryboats included the big *Silver Lake* and *Pamlico*, built at a cost of
over a half-million dollars each; these vessels served the Ocracoke-
Cedar Island route. In a single summer month in 1968, the Bogue
Sound ferries carried 31,000 cars and 85,000 passengers between the
mainland and Emerald Isle.

By 1970 the interstate highway system in North Carolina covered 450 miles. A spectacular 22-mile-long section, opened in 1968,
stretched between Cove Creek in Haywood County to the Tennessee line on Highway I-40. This section, which wound through the

1935 patrol car and trooper. N.C. State Archives. This was the first year in which patrol cars began to replace motorcycles in North Carolina.

Pigeon River Valley, with the river on one side and jagged mountain slopes rising sharply on the other, was a cut blasted out with 125 train carloads of explosives. Other interstate routes connected Virginia and South Carolina across the Coastal Plain (I-95) and Piedmont (I-77) while I-85 swept southwest across the Piedmont through Durham, Greensboro, and Charlotte.

The policing of so large a system of highways, the most extensive state-maintained one in the United States, required the expansion of the State Highway Patrol from the 37 "road sheriffs" who served in 1929 to a force of nearly 900 troopers in 1970. By the latter year the state had 73,000 miles of roads and 2½ million licensed drivers. Yet Morehead City and Wilmington remained the only two major American ports not served by the interstate highway system, and Wilmington still had no four-lane route to promote its development. Nor had North Carolina responded promptly to the opening of the Chesapeake Bay Bridge-Tunnel, which might have directed huge fleets of traffic into the state's tidelands if a suitable North Carolina connection had been provided. Nor for another several decades could North Carolina expect to see its key highway problems solved.

The want of modern access to Wilmington and Morehead City could be seen as a lingering taint of regressive sectionalism. In earlier times, Coastal Plain legislators had gleefully denied advantages to the Piedmont and west; now the Piedmont-dominated General Assembly took its revenge. Bold arteries crisscrossed the Piedmont and snaked with federal aid across the Appalachians—but the main roads stopped well short of the coast. In the panoply of Tar Heel characteristics, sectionalism had outlived provincialism.

The Press Gang

Invigorated by rural free delivery and improved means of transportation, North Carolina's newspapers between 1920 and 1970 improved steadily in quality and increased considerably in size. Newspaper circulation, which passed 2 million in 1926, was led by the city dailies such as the *Charlotte Observer*, Raleigh *News and Observer*, and *Greensboro Daily News*. The number of papers fell as metropolitan dailies encroached on the territory of small-town and rural weeklies. In 1939, for example, the state had 227 papers; by 1960 the figure was down to 194, including 47 dailies. The *Charlotte Observer* captured and held the lead in circulation over its competitors, raising its pressruns to almost a quarter of a million per issue by 1960.

For its relatively poor condition in some respects, North Carolina enjoyed a high reputation for the quality and dynamism of its newspaper press. Josephus Daniels, secretary of the navy and ambassador to Mexico, earned renown for the influence he exercised as editor of the *News and Observer*. His fearlessness extended to attacks on the powerful tobacco and textile interests, which controlled so much of his newspaper's advertising. The chief voice of liberalism in the state in the 1920s was that of Gerald W. Johnson of the *Greensboro Daily News*, an eloquent firebrand who was not infrequently instrumental in directing the drift of popular opinion and the impetus of public policy through his editorials.

Frequently, however, journalistic interest focused not so much on the powerful-but-staid city papers as on the gifted eccentrics who sometimes emerged in the provinces. The most controversial newspaperman in the state during the interwar years was W. O. Saunders, owner and editor of the little Elizabeth City *Independent*, in the far northeastern corner of the state. Saunders was famous for such escapades as parading along New York's Broadway and Fifth Avenue in his pajamas to protest the discomfort of men's summer attire. His blast at a New Deal privy-building program in 1934 was reprinted from coast to coast, and he was an advocate of birth control and abolition of the death penalty when only the lost and despised could be so. Ordered by the courts to retract a headline calling a Pasquotank County man "An Ass," Saunders gleefully heralded in yet bolder type the revelation that the man was "Not an Ass." In a moment of high editorial drama in 1924, he emblazoned his front page with the opinion that a popular visiting revivalist/evangelist was a liar and brought down the wrath of the whole community on his head. But Saunders survived to record his opinions not only in his own paper but also in *Collier's*, *American Magazine*, and other national publications.

Less provocative but equally interesting was Louis Graves's *Chapel Hill Weekly*. Graves, an Orange County native formerly em-

Josephus Daniels (1862–1948). Duke University Manuscript Department.

W. O. Saunders attacked Mordecai Ham, an anti-Semitic revivalist who held a revival in Elizabeth City in 1924. Ham reviled Julius Rosenwald of Sears, Roebuck and Company and accused Jews of plotting the destruction of gentile civilization. Saunders called Ham "a charlatan, a four-flusher and a liar." In Saunders's *Book of Ham* he explained: "The Prophet Ham came to Elizabeth City to dynamite Hell out of Elizabeth City. In the course of events it became necessary for me to dynamite a little Hell out of Ham."

ployed by the *New York Times*, inaugurated his Chapel Hill paper in 1923. His ability to write engagingly about the foibles of day-to-day existence enabled him to give the *Weekly* a folksy, chatty style that caught on with the egghead community and flourished amid the competition of the Durham and Raleigh dailies. A cat rescued from a tree, the burning question of whether dogs should be allowed to roam freely on the University of North Carolina campus, a raid by chickens on a backyard garden—such was the stuff of an essayist's delight in Graves's skilled hands. By 1949 a panegyrist could declare that the paper was "as much of a State institution as the University of North Carolina."

William Oscar Saunders (1908–37). N.C. State Archives.

Many Tar Heel journalists went on to national prominence in both the newspaper and television fields: Wilmington's David Brinkley with NBC, Greensboro's Edward R. Murrow with CBS, Raleigh's Vermont Royster with the *Wall Street Journal*, Hamlet's Tom Wicker and Zebulon's Clifton Daniel with the *New York Times*. Some who stayed behind also achieved national recognition, as when W. Horace Carter of the *Tabor City Tribune* won a Pulitzer Prize in 1952 for his editorials against the Ku Klux Klan. It was the first time the award had ever gone to a weekly paper, though the semiweekly Whiteville *News Reporter* took a Pulitzer in 1953.

North Carolina's magazines, however, fared ill in the century's middle decades. The *North Carolina University Magazine* was discontinued in 1920 after three quarters of a century of publication and was soon followed into eclipse by the *North Carolina Booklet*, which was directed at state-history buffs. Subsidized journals such as Duke University's *South Atlantic Quarterly* and the state-published *North Carolina Historical Review* (founded in 1924) weathered depression and popular indifference, but unsubsidized ventures nearly always ended in failure. The *State*, a Raleigh magazine created in 1933 by journalist Carl Goerch, managed to withstand the tides of adversity by incorporating a mixture of personality profiles, down-home lore, and sketches of this and that sort of North Caroliniana.

An exception to the rule of periodical lethargy was Clarence Poe's *Progressive Farmer*. Poe took over what was then a small farm newspaper in 1899 when he was an eighteen-year-old with no college background. His blend of practical, down-to-earth matter directed at farmers and their families touched a popular chord and built the *Progressive Farmer* into one of the world's great mass-circulation farm journals. *Golf World* was a Southern Pines publication with a national following, the *North Carolina Folklore Journal* a Raleigh periodical of more limited appeal.

Nell Battle Lewis (1893?–1956) made a name in journalism, writing for the Raleigh *News and Observer* and other publications. She championed progressive stands on public welfare, politics, education, and women's rights while attacking institutions and traditional values that trammeled individual freedom and the inquiring mind.

Air Ways

The integration of North Carolina's once-fragmented provinces and sections was not due entirely to better highways and the periodical press. It also owed something to the expansion of telephone and radio service, the introduction and development of television and the airplane, and the role of railroads.

In 1920 the railroad was still, as it had been for three quarters of a century, the workhorse of the state's public transportation. But railroads were soon to feel injury from the competition of more flexible trucks and buses and speedier airplanes. The spread of automobile ownership did further harm to railroads. Moreover, North Carolina travelers found the main north-south routes awkward because the

Club car of the Crescent Queen, 1949.
N.C. State Archives. This train ran between New York and New Orleans.

schedules served the convenience of passengers boarding in the metropolitan Northeast or the Deep South. East-west rail routes, never well developed in North Carolina, generated only sporadic traffic, even to the port towns of Morehead City and Wilmington.

What the railroads did well—the rapid transit of overland bulk cargoes—they were unrivaled in. The three routes by which the Norfolk & Western fed coal to the industrial Piedmont carried nearly 6½ million tons—or 91,000 carloads—in 1970. Also brought into the state by the Norfolk & Western were some 200,000 cars and trucks, many of which were unloaded and stored temporarily at the company's 5,600-vehicle lot at Walkertown. Carried along the same routes were nearly 3,000 carloads of furniture as well as grain, beer, paper and printed material, food products, and much else. The three largest railroads that served North Carolina in 1970—the South-ern Railway, the Norfolk & Southern, and the Seaboard Coast Line —were important to the state's economic well-being, but not in proportion to their importance half a century before.

Commercial air service was not a significant factor in North Carolina until World War II. As late as 1960 the state in which aviation began had only six airports with scheduled air-carrier service. Legis-lative foot-dragging on the subject of airport construction meant that between 1962 and 1966 North Carolina received less than 3 percent of the federal funds allocated for that purpose among seven southern states. A tardy but vigorous response to the mounting need was bringing improvement as the decade of the 1960s ended.

In 1970 North Carolina had thirteen airports with scheduled service. The busiest of these was Douglas Airport at Charlotte, which was served by five airlines; Greensboro-High Point, Raleigh-

Piedmont Airlines DC-3 Pacemaker. N.C. State Archives.

Warf's Airport, Reidsville, Rockingham County, resembles a typical facility in the early days of air transportation.

Railroad bridge in the mountains.

1919 dial telephone. All telephone pictures courtesy American Telephone and Telegraph Company.

(Center) 1928 desk telephone.

(Right) 1937 "300" type desk set telephone.

Durham, and Asheville were each served by three lines. A total of twelve airports in the state were served by the largest of the intrastate carriers, Piedmont Airlines of Winston-Salem. Douglas and Raleigh-Durham each handled well over half a million passengers and over four hundred daily operations in 1967, and these figures were expected to double by 1971. But airport managers and others close to the situation foresaw trouble unless much larger funds were soon made available for the vast physical requirements of the dawning big-jet era. The route to Heaven itself, in the view of many Tar Heels, probably meant changing in Atlanta.

Urban public transportation evolved from the horsecar to the trolley car to the city bus, but the popularity of the automobile made buses generally a losing proposition for city taxpayers. More successful financially were the interstate and intercity lines such as Greyhound and Carolina Trailways. The latter was a Raleigh-based firm that began in 1925 with routes between Raleigh and towns within a radius of about 75 miles. Later, Carolina Trailways was a charter member of the national organization known as Nationwide Trailways. By 1966 Carolina Trailways, through the development of new routes and the purchase of rights to existing ones, had terminals in five states and a fleet of 240 buses. In that year the line logged 23 million miles and carried 5.7 million passengers. In the intervening years, it had evolved a wide range of one-stop or nonstop routes to as far away as New York City, and its buses had been equipped with air conditioning, lavatories, and other modern conveniences.

Commercial radio broadcasting began in North Carolina in 1922 when a license was issued to WBT in Charlotte. Earle Gluck, one of the organizers of the station, had earlier operated an experimental station from a private home in Charlotte, transmitting from an abandoned chicken house. The chief innovator among the early stations, however, was the next one established: WPTF in Raleigh. WPTF won renown for its "firsts" in Tar Heel broadcasting, including football and basketball games, live broadcasts from the State Fair, and a regularly scheduled farm program. By 1971 there were 231 commercial

(Left) 1949 "500" type desk set telephone.

(Center) 1959 "Princess" telephone.

(Above) 1968 12-button touch-tone telephone.

and noncommercial radio stations operating in the state, an increase of about 25 percent over the previous decade.

The era of commercial television in North Carolina was inaugurated in July 1949 by WBTV in Charlotte, followed within weeks by WFMY-TV in Greensboro. Within three decades more than 90 percent of the homes in the state had TV sets, and there were fifteen commercial and three educational stations. The North Carolina Association of Broadcasters was the fifth largest such organization in the country, and the influence of the television medium was attested in 1972 when Tar Heel TV commentator Jesse Helms won nomination and election to the United States Senate.

Telephones were a nineteenth-century invention, but their widespread use came slowly to North Carolina. There were only 179,000 in use in the state in 1939 and not yet twice that many in 1947. During the next few years, however, telephone lines were extended into many rural areas previously without them; by 1960 there were well over 1 million telephones in the state—and the number was increasing rapidly. By 1969 Southern Bell alone, largest of the state's twenty-four companies, had more than 1 million telephones in operation, though there were many rural families who still lacked the service.

Linked ear-to-ear by telephone; connected town-to-town by road and rail; attuned to the pulse of the nation and the world through newspapers, interstate highways, jet planes, and network broadcasting, their views and activities rehearsed and analyzed hour-by-hour on radio and television, North Carolinians entered the decade of the 1970s far more aware than ever before of the world within as well as the world beyond. A new, more cosmopolitan Tar Heel personality was emerging in spite of late efforts to preserve what was wholesome in the traditional personality. It seemed likely that, for good or ill, the North Carolinian of the year 2000 would be a stranger to his 1920 predecessor.

Robert Simpson described the changed scene: "Back in the late fifties an' early sixties the U.S. economy was boomin' an' there were jobs available everywhere. . . . But the town has changed a lot now. They're movin' stores out to the highway an' puttin' up these big shoppin' centers, an' the trains don't run through like they used to. . . . We're still a small town . . . but things are definitely less personal, y'know? Even in little ol' Rose Hill, North Carolina, nothin' is goin' to be the same." Wolcott, *Rose Hill.*

Mordecai Ham (1877–1961). *50 Years
on the Battle Front with Christ*, in the
N.C. State Library. Ham's efforts were
successful at a Charlotte tent meeting in
1934. William ("Billy") F. Graham, then
aged seventeen, heard him and was
convinced.

84

The Desert Blooms

"Evilution"

The year 1920 saw North Carolina reeling dolefully toward a dreaded showdown between conflicting factions of its cultural and intellectual leadership. A small but earnest and vocal element was concerned about the threat to traditional values posed by the whirlwind of new ideas and gadgets of the past generation or so. Another group, similarly articulate and committed, conceived of itself as precursors of a bright new world that would be safe for novel gadgets and ideas. By 1920 it was becoming clear that the two groups had settled upon evolutionary science as the central issue over which they would first test their relative strength.

Evolution was wonderfully designed to crystallize a thousand differences on other matters. Bewitchingly inviting to the rationalist mentality, it seemed from the perspective of the biblical literalists a thing of sin and sacrilege. Those who favored the Darwinian scheme of things also were perceived by their critics as tolerant of socialism and unionism, permissive toward sexual behavior, sympathetic to the rights of women and minorities, and so on. Those arrayed against Darwinism tended to oppose these and related views. The first group was called "liberal," the second "conservative." Most Tar Heels were not strictly identifiable with either group, but the tug of centuries of sentiment drew them more toward the latter.

In North Carolina the issue between the two groups reached a crisis in the mid-1920s. Focal points in the ensuing struggle included W. O. Saunders's furious combat against evangelist Mordecai Ham in Elizabeth City in the fall of 1924 and an effort by fundamentalists to oust from office Dr. William L. Poteat, proevolutionist president of Wake Forest College, the state's leading Baptist school. (Governor Morrison personally banned two textbooks from the public schools because they taught evolution.)

In early 1925 a bill to prohibit the teaching of evolution in the public schools was introduced in the state legislature. The so-called "Poole bill" failed by one vote to win the endorsement of the Education Committee and went on to defeat on the floor of the House. By this margin was North Carolina spared the humiliation of another Scopes trial.

The fate of the Poole bill, coupled with a successful defense of Dr. Poteat, beguiled the liberal faction into unwarranted self-confidence. Politically, North Carolina remained safely under moderately conservative government throughout the interwar years and for some time thereafter. The overwhelming majority of public-school teachers shunned the subject of evolution in the classroom. Sexual emancipation, unionism, theological liberalism, and other tenets of the modernists found little acceptance among Tar Heels. In 1934 Mordecai Ham, at a tent meeting outside Charlotte, took his revenge on the evolutionists by planting the spark of spiritual rebirth into the bosom of a farm lad named Billy Graham.

The fragility of the liberal position was made manifest in 1950 with the defeat of Frank Porter Graham, moderately liberal president of the University of North Carolina, in his bid for nomination by the Democratic party as its candidate for the United States Senate. Scion of an old and respected family, well-known across the state and nation, strongly backed by a popular governor, Graham was beaten by Raleigh Attorney Willis Smith, a solid conservative. The campaign was marked by vicious calumnies that portrayed Graham as a "nigger-lover" who was soft on Communism. More than any election in many years, the senatorial primary of 1950 pitted liberal and conservative viewpoints in stark confrontation.

Still another round in the running dispute occurred in 1963 over the "Speaker-Ban Law." Alarmed by noisy student civil rights demonstrations in Greensboro, Chapel Hill, and elsewhere, conservative legislators drafted a bill to impose restrictions on visiting speakers who made use of state property. Passage of the act raised a pained outcry from the academic community, then far more populous than in the 1920s. Anxious to find a peaceful resolution, Governor Moore appointed a study commission, which recommended certain modifications of the law. Authority over visiting speakers was ultimately returned to the state campuses, but it required an order of a federal district court to abrogate the Speaker-Ban Law as unconstitutional.

Again, the Tar Heel liberal element had won a victory that smacked more of symbol than substance. Skeptics had only to observe the state's grudging response to court-ordered public school desegregation to understand that North Carolinians remained largely committed to conservative values.

Lunch at Woolworth's

In contrast with more militant states of the Deep South, North Carolina in the mid-twentieth century found itself with an unwonted reputation for moderation. No fire-eating Tar Heel senator raged against New Deal policies, no spokesman for the state made himself conspicuous as a "nigger-baiter" or patriotic witch-hunter. As in the 1850s, some saw North Carolina as a potentially valuable happy medium between the extremes of North and South—a reconciler and healer of divisions, capable of helping to bind the sections of the Union more closely together. That the state was unprepared to shoulder such a burden was soon to become as evident in regard to the issues of the twentieth century as it had been concerning those of the nineteenth.

Following the Supreme Court's desegregation decision in 1954, Governor William B. Umstead appointed an Advisory Committee on Education to deal with the problems the decision posed for the state's long-segregated public school system. Umstead shortly thereafter died in office, but the committee's proposals were adopted by his successor, former Lieutenant Governor Luther Hodges. What the committee recommended was that desegregation be approached by means of a locally controlled pupil assignment plan. By an act of the

Sit-in at Woolworth's lunch counter, 1 February 1960. *Greensboro Record*. The building, now empty, still stands, on Market Street, Greensboro, Guilford County.

Civil-rights demonstrators outside the K and W Cafeteria in Winston-Salem, Forsyth County, 6 June 1963. *Winston-Salem Journal-Sentinel*.

Cartoon by Hugh Haynie. *Greensboro Daily News*.

General Assembly of 1955, parents wishing their children reassigned to a segregated school of the other race had to go through an almost prohibitively complicated application procedure. Theoretically, this so-called "Pearsall Plan" might have thwarted any desegregation at all, but this, according to its sponsors, was not its purpose.

North Carolina's white leaders sought no "massive resistance" to the federal government. The Pearsall Plan would permit a handful of black children to attend previously all-white schools, resulting in

Ku Klux Klan rally, 1964. N.C. State Archives.

Brady's Restaurant sit-in, 1964, in Chapel Hill, Orange County. N.C. State Archives.

Sit-ins were tried without publicity as early as 1943. In 1957 seven students, led by the Reverend Douglas E. Moore of Asbury Temple Methodist Church, went in the white entrance and took seats at the Royal Ice Cream Company, at Roxboro and Dowd streets, Durham. They were arrested and fined twenty-five dollars each.

the desegregation of perhaps 1 percent or less of the school system. Token compliance with the federal government was supposed to accomplish two things: it would keep the hounds of integration effectively at bay and would prevent a "red-neck" backlash that might well destroy the public schools. Evidence that such a rebellion might actually occur was lacking, but the possibility seemed enough to legitimize the Pearsall Plan. The Pearsall scheme also contributed to North Carolina's image as a moderate state with wholesome racial relations.

Kress building, Market Street, Greensboro, Guilford County. Photograph by Joann Sieburg-Baker. N.C. State Archives. Besides its connection with the sit-ins of the 1960s, this building is distinguished by the art deco style of architecture of the 1920s and '30s.

Black frustration over the state's foot-dragging on desegregation was one of the factors behind the protest movement that began in Greensboro on 1 February 1960. On that day, four students from all-black North Carolina Agricultural and Technical College sat down at a lunch counter in the Woolworth's department store and asked for service. Refused on the ground that local custom forbade it, the students occupied their seats until closing time and returned the next day with reinforcements. In subsequent days they were joined by others, including a few white students. When the Woolworth counter was fully occupied by protesters, others moved on the S. H. Kress store down the street.

Sit-ins had occurred at other places throughout the country in earlier years, but those in Greensboro became the tocsin of social revolution. A week later they had spread to Winston-Salem and Durham, the seats of other black colleges. Within two weeks they were occurring in other states and touching off sympathetic demonstrations in the North. When the Woolworth, Kress, and Myers stores in Greensboro relented in July and allowed blacks to eat at their lunch counters, it seemed that the seas had parted at last for the black community. The commotion had called forth another resurgence of the Ku Klux Klan (as well as the Speaker Ban), but it had also produced a dynamic and charismatic new black leader, A & T College football star Jesse Jackson.

And yet, the sit-in victory was in some respects a hollow one. The right to eat lunch in a department store was not, after all, the American dream. It carried with it no political power, no economic clout, no access to better housing or better jobs. It did nothing to improve educational opportunity for blacks still victimized by the Pearsall Plan. Greensboro's white leaders, like many elsewhere in the state and region, for the most part submitted reluctantly to the Civil Rights Act of 1964, the Supreme Court's ruling against "freedom of choice" plans in 1967, and other federal initiatives. The sit-ins had raised expectations among blacks that were not to be fulfilled in the lifetimes of many of their participants. Nevertheless, they were a start, and this first small step was crucial.

Rebel Rib

The decade of the 1920s opened with the Nineteenth Amendment on the verge of adoption and North Carolina in position to be the state to guarantee the enfranchisement of women. But, amid warnings that "politics are bad for women and women for politics," the state legislature rejected the amendment, and Tennessee next day provided the last vote needed for ratification.

Equality of status, nevertheless, continued to elude the Tar Heel woman throughout the fifty-year period; only after World War II would she gain the right to sue and recover for personal injuries, to keep her earnings and property separate, and to dispose of her real property without her husband's consent. Even so, there remained numerous realms in which women were accorded inferior legal status.

Some continued to defend the legal double standard as providing as much in protection for women as in limitation. It was the husband, after all, and not the wife, who was required by law to support a couple's children. A husband must pay for his wife's funeral expenses but not vice versa. Criminal conduct was found in a man who peeped through a bedroom window at a disrobing woman, but not when a woman peeped at a man.

Such distinctions had their origin and rationale in an age in which women rarely held jobs outside the home. And this pattern held true in North Carolina until the era of World War II, when large numbers of women took jobs formerly held by men. Many returned home with the coming of peace, but the demonstrated ability of women to perform well many jobs previously reserved for men helped to kindle the spark of ambition in the younger generation of North Carolina womanhood.

Changes in education facilitated the fulfillment of these ambitions. The University of North Carolina opened its first housing for women students in 1921. Despite opposition from the male students ("Women Not Wanted Here" thundered the *Daily Tar Heel*), the university opened a women's dormitory in 1925, a year after awarding its first doctoral degrees to women. The state's "Woman's College" remained sexually segregated until 1965, when it was renamed the University of North Carolina at Greensboro. By 1972 women made up almost 40 percent of the student body at Chapel Hill and were rapidly overtaking the men. For many years before this, Tar Heel men had trailed women by about a year in average formal education.

Role models for the emancipated generation of women were provided by a small number of female doctors, lawyers, nurses, suffragettes, and others. A notable standard of achievement in this era was the career of Charlotte Hawkins Brown, a Vance County native. The daughter of former slaves, Mrs. Brown was educated at Wellesley College, in Massachusetts, and returned to North Carolina in 1902 with a missionary zeal to devote her life to the improvement of the lives of black people. The school she founded in Guilford County, Palmer Memorial Institute, gradually gained strength and recognition as a private elementary and high school for black children.

The school, however, was only one of the many-sided contributions of its founder. Mrs. Brown published a novel of black life in

One observer of the social scene saw changes during the period as results of the women's movement: "Rural society was, and remained, pretty much static until the advent of good roads, the automobile, birth control, more leisure, and more careers for women. It was, at length, the women who rebelled. Men were for the most part satisfied with the status quo. The restless, educated female, resentful of conventions and restraints, inspired by freedom gained during two world wars, brought man's world crashing over his head, thus precipitating a reorientation of the solid social structure of the horse-and-buggy era." Taylor, *Carolina Crossroads*.

Charlotte Hawkins Brown (1883–1961). N.C. State Archives.

Susie Marshall Sharp, born in Rocky Mount in 1907, shown as an associate justice of the North Carolina Supreme Court, 1962. N.C. State Archives.

1919 (the first of her several books) and helped to organize the North Carolina Federation of Women's Clubs and the Colored Orphanage at Oxford. The Home Ownership Association, which she helped to launch at Sedalia, is credited with increasing home ownership there from 2 percent to 95 percent by 1930. Before her death in 1961, she had been awarded four honorary doctorates and many other awards and distinctions.

A beacon to those interested in a larger role for women in public affairs was the career of Ellen Black Winston. Born in Bryson City, she earned a doctorate at the University of Chicago in 1930. After teaching at Meredith College in Raleigh in the early 1940s, she became the state's commissioner of public welfare in 1944, a post she held for nineteen years. Dr. Winston also served terms in the 1950s and 1960s as president of the American Welfare Association and National Conference for Social Service. The capstone of her career was her appointment in 1963 as commissioner of public welfare for the U.S. Department of Health, Education, and Welfare. Dr. Winston was also a United States representative on the United Nations' International Conference of Ministers of Social Welfare.

Susie Marshall Sharp, a Reidsville lawyer, enjoyed the distinction of serving as a justice on the North Carolina Supreme Court at a time when few women obtained law degrees. A graduate of the University of North Carolina law school and editor there of its law review, she became the first woman appointed judge of the Superior Court. In 1974 she was elected chief justice of the state supreme court by the largest majority on the Democratic ticket, the first woman to attain so high a judicial position.

Fields of Glory

As Rome was hellenized by its conquest of Greece, so the twentieth-century city fell cultural captive to its rural vassals. The first generation or two of migrants from the "branch-heads" might experience misgivings about city life, but three centuries of rural Tar Heel culture proved highly resistant to asphalt and acetylene. Gradually, country people learned to soften the geometrical contours of the city and tame it into livability. The Chamber Music Guild survived, but it learned a new respect for Bluegrass and Country.

An intriguing example of the vitality of rural culture was the half-century's religious experience. North Carolina in colonial times had been widely considered lost and perhaps unredeemable. But the Great Revival at the opening of the nineteenth century welded the people of the state firmly into the Bible Belt. Church membership outstripped population growth. By 1926 the state's sixty-seven religious denominations enrolled half of all North Carolinians. The huge majority of church members were Protestant and the great proportion of these were Baptists, with Methodists and Presbyterians trailing well behind. Overwhelmingly, the churches of the 1920s were small rural affairs averaging about a hundred members each.

On rare occasions, as in the struggle over Darwinism in the mid-1920s, the country churches could be marshaled into strong coordinated activity. This was also true of the 1928 presidential campaign when the Democrats sponsored an anti-Prohibitionist Roman Catholic. Many southern Protestant clergy campaigned actively against Al Smith in the most widespread social agitation since the Populist revolt. But these were exceptional instances, and the country church normally exerted its influence on a local and personal level rather than a state or regional one. For this reason, the profound social impact of the rural church was often unnoticed by the urban-centered social analyst.

A survey of North Carolina's churches in 1929 noted with dismay the number of rural institutions found to be discontinued or abandoned. "Enthusiasm in many of the country churches," a commentator observed, "is gone, hope is waning, members are leaving, and the churches are dying." Observers sometimes jumped from such a discovery to the conclusion that religion itself was threatened. But the waning of the small, rural edifice did not portend a decline of religious interest or activity. In this transitional epoch, the ruralist-turned-urbanite was feeling his way toward an accommodation of his religious ideas to his city life.

In the contest of rural and urban religious values, it was not infrequently the former that emerged victorious. One result was the rise of big new churches near or within the fringes of urban centers. These institutions, directed by ardently evangelistic leaders, combined the modern facilities and bus fleets of the sophisticated municipal churches with the forcefully biblical impulses of the inspired rural congregations. The new churches, urban in appearance but rural in character, were often strong enough to enable their members to resist the intense forces of social reform after World War II. Church-operated day-care centers, schools, and Sunday schools preserved the rural heritage amid the clamor of social upheaval.

The wedding of rural evangelicalism with urban electronic media produced spectacular results. Instead of being tamed into urbane blandness, the evangelicals found vast new audiences for their appeals. The obstacles of poor roads and isolated congregations overcome by technology, the best evangelistic preachers became extraordinarily effective radio and TV sermonizers. A prodigy of the new mass-appeal approach was Charlotte's William Franklin ("Billy") Graham.

Two experiences seem to have been profoundly important in Billy Graham's early development. One was his own "decision for Christ" at a 1934 evangelistic tent meeting. The other was a highly successful stint as a summer Fuller Brush salesman following his graduation from high school. After taking his college degree at Wheaton, Graham for a time was only a moderately successful "sawdust trail Bible-thumper." But a "Crusade for Christ" he led in Los Angeles in 1949 transformed him into a national figure and a personality of magnetic self-confidence.

Graham's career was propelled forward by a number of conversions of well-known people at his Los Angeles crusade. In the next five years, he perfected his publicity techniques and toned down the fierce emotional rant of his earlier days. By the time his crusade hit New York in 1957, Graham was a smooth and polished media celebrity. In less than four months in New York, he spoke before well over two million people and claimed more than sixty thousand conversions. By then he regularly preached on his "Hour of Decision" radio program and wrote a syndicated newspaper column. He would later add a monthly magazine to his international media campaign, along with recordings, leaflets, and thirteen books written by himself. In the meantime, his crusades were further moderated in tone, be-

William ("Billy") Graham. Courtesy Durham Herald Company.

coming, in the words of one critic, "less like . . . a circus and more like . . . a cathedral."

Once as conservative and super-patriotic as others in his theological mold, Graham racially integrated his crusade audiences in the early 1950s. Strongly emphasizing the need for individual regeneration, he did not scorn social reform. From his wide travels around the world and his contacts with the world's movers and shakers, he seemed to acquire increasing tolerance and breadth of vision. Scores of others adopted his techniques in the 1950s and 1960s, but none so effectively as their originator.

If the new evangelicals made a marked impression on personal morality among Tar Heels, they did not retard the exuberant flowering of popular recreation and entertainment. The filling of leisure time with suitable activities and spectacles became the basis of a number of major industries in North Carolina. Easily the most successful of these in the middle decades of the century were spectator sports.

Big-time football was the earliest of the era's athletic spectacles. By the 1920s the larger colleges had developed keen rivalries in various sports, but the people's choice was clearly the fast and rugged action of the gridiron. A contest between the universities of North Carolina and Virginia was, besides, a chance to even the score against generations of Old Dominion "witlings," as the state song phrased it, who had "defamed" and "sneered at" their less fortunate neighbors. But it was the Wallace Wade powerhouses at Duke in the 1930s and 1940s that brought national attention to North Carolina and gave football firm claim to center stage.

The participation of two Wade teams in Rose Bowls, the marvel of his unscored-on 1939 team, and the renown of stars such as "Ace" Parker and George McAfee made Duke a catalyst for rival schools in the state. The University of North Carolina recovered its dignity in the late 1940s behind the all-around prowess of Charlie ("Choo-Choo") Justice, but the teams of the state and region were not generally competitive with those of other parts of the country after Wade's glory years. Then too, football lost some measure of its prominence after World War II when North Carolina State College hired for its new basketball coach a high-school coach from Indiana named Everett Case.

Case brought down several outstanding Indiana players with him and proceeded to convert North Carolina into "basketball country." The major teams in the state in 1949 put together a tournament known as the "Dixie Classic," which was for years the outstanding spectator attraction in North Carolina. (It was abolished in the 1960s because of the discovery of criminal involvement in it.) Wake Forest responded to Case's challenge with excellent teams of its own, coached by Pamlico County's "Bones" McKinney and featuring such local talent as All-American center Dickie Hemric of Jonesville.

Wallace Wade watching his team play. Duke University Archives. Relaxed and arrayed in a business suit, Wade presents a contrast to today's coaches, who pace the sidelines in sports coats and anxiously mastermind the plays.

95

Maxine Allen. N.C. State Archives.

(Right) Al Attles holds the 1959 CIAA Basketball Championship trophy. Courtesy North Carolina Agricultural and Technical State University.

Junior Johnson and Cale Yarborough. Courtesy Charlotte Motor Speedway.

Duke guard Dick Groat brought luster to the program at that school, while coach Frank McGuire's undefeated 1957 national champions ignited a long era of basketball fanaticism at Chapel Hill. Al Attles of A & T and Earl Monroe of Winston-Salem State were among the splendid products of the black schools. Unlike football, the state's basketball teams after the 1940s were competitive with the best of those in any region of the country.

Baseball, which enjoyed a popularity independent of the college rivalries, nevertheless (or therefore) failed to maintain its reputation as the "national pastime." Numerous Tar Heels went on to celebrity in the major leagues, notably brothers Rick and Wes Ferrell of Durham (Rick as a catcher and Wes as a pitcher), infielder Billy Goodman of Concord, pitcher Johnny Allen of Lenoir, Enos ("Country") Slaughter of Roxboro, and, in the Negro National League, outfielder Buck Leonard of Rocky Mount. But baseball was a way to while away an hour or two rather than a focus of popular enthusiasm.

Other sports ranked generally well behind these in popularity. Maxine Allen of Seaboard became the leading women's duck-pin bowler in the nation in 1952 and, later, a top ten-pin bowler. Charlotte's Jim Beattie set a world's record (3:58.9) in the mile run in 1962, and Morganton's Billy Joe Patton and Tarboro's Harvie Ward became nationally known golfers. But these sports ranked not much ahead of lacrosse, soccer, and pocket billiards (in which Elizabeth City's Luther Lassiter was three times world champion in the 1960s) in spectator appeal for Tar Heels.

Outside the college area, the sports phenomenon of the post-World War II epoch was unquestionably stock-car racing. The sport originated in the 1930s among groups of bootleg-runners and shade-tree mechanics and developed rapidly after the war. By 1949, when Grand National racing with late-model cars began at the Charlotte Motor Speedway, stock cars were a regional addition. The thrill of high speeds and flaming crashes led to such institutionalized tire-burners as the Charlotte 600 and National 500, both of which began in 1960. Within a few years, the North Carolina Motor Speedway at Rockingham added the Carolina 500 and the American 500 to the Grand National tour. But there were many smaller tracks all over the state. Big prize money and the opiate of mortal danger brought forth numbers of drivers eager to test their machinery and engineering skill against one another.

Stock cars made living legends of boys like Junior Johnson of Ronda. Johnson was a bootleg-runner who, before joining the stock-car circuit in 1954, had done a stint in prison after being arrested for manufacturing illicit whiskey. "Instead of going into the curves and just sliding and holding on for dear life like the other drivers," says writer Tom Wolfe, "Junior developed the technique of throwing himself into a slide about seventy-five feet before the curve by cocking the wheel to the left slightly and gunning it, using the slide, not the brake, to slow down, so that he could pick up speed again halfway through the curve and come out of it like a shot. This was known as the 'power slide,' and—yes! of course!—every good old boy in North Carolina started saying Junior Johnson learned that stunt doing those goddamned *about-faces* running away from the Alcohol Tax agents."

Johnson retired in 1966, but Richard Petty of Level Cross, NASCAR's "Rookie of the Year" in 1964, was already emerging as the new nonpareil "king of the road." Following in the steps of his father, stock-car pioneer Lee Petty, Richard in 1972 won his fourth Grand National championship, becoming the first driver in the history of the business to win over a million dollars. Like Johnson, Petty was a folk hero before his thirtieth birthday.

Individual sports such as golf and tennis, once the preserve of the country-club set, grew as municipalities provided public links and courts. The Southern Pines and Pinehurst areas had long provided outstanding golf facilities for tourists and wealthy visitors from out of state, but it was only after World War II that golfing became a weekly recreation for numbers of professional people. Skiing, often on artificial snow, gained a following at Beech Mountain and other Blue Ridge slopes. And sport fishing, from mountain stream to continental shelf, became a major activity among all types and classes of Tar Heels.

National 500 at the Charlotte Motor Speedway, Harrisburg, Cabarrus County. Courtesy Charlotte Motor Speedway. The appeal of these races is partly based on the meaning of the car: "Freedom wasn't some abstract thing being watched over off in Washington. Hell, freedom was the car. . . . And that was never truer than it was in the South after the Second World War when for the first time it was possible for even poor country people to have cars." Bledsoe, *The World's Number One, Flat-Out, All-Time Great Stock Car Racing Book.*

Katherine Clark Pendleton Arrington (1876–1955). N.C. State Archives. Through her work for the North Carolina State Art Society, Mrs. Arrington was instrumental in the establishment of the Mint Museum of Art at Charlotte in 1936, as well as of the State Art Museum at Raleigh in 1956.

Weymouth, the home of James Boyd, Southern Pines, Moore County, is both a nature preserve of virgin pines and a cultural center for the encouragement of the arts and humanities.

Madonna and Child, marble relief by Ferdinand di Simone Ferrucci (1437–93). Kress Collection, North Carolina Museum of Art.

Laurels at Last

A unique institution in North Carolina was the annual late-fall Culture Week, when various statewide organizations devoted to history, literature, and the arts held meetings in Raleigh. It was during Culture Week that those groups sponsoring awards for meritorious Tar Heel work in cultural endeavors announced their winners. The Mayflower Cup, for example, was presented for the best work of nonfiction, the Sir Walter Award for the finest work of fiction, the Roanoke-Chowan Poetry Award for the outstanding book of poetry. Whether Culture Week added incentive or inspiration to cultural achievement in North Carolina was open to question, but it did symbolize the desire of many Tar Heels to recognize those of special talent or distinction.

Although it lacked a long tradition of important contribution to art and letters, North Carolina in the 1920s experienced a significant cultural awakening. Polkville's Hatcher Hughes won the Pulitzer Prize in 1924 for his folk drama *Hell-Bent for Heaven*, and Lillington's Paul Green won it in 1927 for his play *In Abraham's Bosom*. A series of novels by James Boyd of Southern Pines won critical and popular success in the 1920s and 1930s. Lamar Stringfield of Raleigh won the Pulitzer Prize in music with his suite *From the Southern Mountains*, and Hunter Johnson earned the *Prix de Rome* in 1938 for his musical compositions. Meanwhile, Thomas Wolfe's novels and Howard Odum's studies in the sociology of the South had been gaining a worldwide audience.

The state had no such institution as a genuine art museum until 1936, when Charlotte's Mint Museum of Art was established. Hickory's museum of art was organized eight years later, but these were the only two such institutions in North Carolina at the close of World War II. The North Carolina Art Society, recipient after 1929 of limited public funds, established a small museum in a room at the State Agricultural Building—but painting was the exotic interest of the few as the decade of the 1950s began.

An improbable proposal to inaugurate a state art gallery emerged in the General Assembly during World War II and for a number of years lurked in the shadows of indifference and derision. In 1951 an offer by New York mercantile tycoon S. H. Kress to donate a million dollars worth of art to the state on a matching basis galvanized interest in the project. New efforts in the legislature produced money with which to acquire the Kress Collection and convert the old Highway Building in Raleigh into an art gallery. In 1956 the North Carolina Museum of Art opened its doors and ultimately evolved into one of the nation's major museums. But the private sector was also astir with new energies in behalf of art. Asheville, Statesville, and Chapel Hill acquired museums between 1948 and 1958, lending artistic credibility to one of the states comprising a region that had formerly been, in H. L. Mencken's harsh indictment, the "Sahara of the Bozart."

State funds also gave impetus to the North Carolina Symphony, which was founded in 1933 as the first state symphony in the nation. Several energetic local groups such as the Friends of the College at North Carolina State University promoted ambitious programs by

The North Carolina Symphony, conducted by John Gosling, shown performing in Memorial Auditorium, Raleigh. Courtesy North Carolina Symphony. Despite a state subsidy to defray expenses, for many years the musicians donated their services. Under the guidance of musical directors Benjamin Swalin and John Gosling the organization has achieved the professional competence it possesses today.

The educational impetus in North Carolina under Governor Sanford (1961–65) resulted in two innovative schools: The North Carolina School for the Performing Arts, Winston-Salem, Forsyth County, and the Governor's School, a summer program for gifted high school students at Salem College, Winston-Salem, and St. Andrews College, Laurinburg, Scotland County.

visiting performers, and the North Carolina School of the Performing Arts at Winston-Salem became an important training center for young musicians and other artists. An inventory in the late 1960s enumerated seventeen symphony orchestras and concert groups across the state, as well as seventeen community arts councils, sixty-four display centers for art, sixty-five theater groups, and seventy-four concert series. The appropriation for the arts of $1.8 million by the legislature for 1966 alone denoted a strong public commitment to the state's cultural life.

Private support for the arts likewise expanded impressively. A group of banks in 1967 sponsored a tour of the schools in the state by a Shakespearean company. Corporate contributions figured heavily in the founding of the Raleigh Little Theatre in 1964, the Grass Roots Opera Company (later the National Opera Company) in Raleigh in 1948, and other cultural ventures. Meanwhile, the burgeoning growth of outdoor drama had brought cultural enrichment to thousands in the hinterlands.

The Social Organism

Implicit in the transformation of cultural life in North Carolina was a recognition that it was not enough for Tar Heels to come to terms with the rest of the region, the nation, the world. They must also come to terms with each other. No age demanded this recognition more insistently.

The pressure for minority rights for blacks, women, children, the aged, and the poor were so many reminders of an ancient but evidently doomed social and sexual hierarchy. Conceivably, some new hierarchy was emerging to replace it. But hierarchy itself was in ill-repute. The American Indian rejected ascriptions of inferiority. Advocates of migrant laborers appeared in North Carolina courtrooms. The handicapped won recognition of their right to ramps and other special facilities in public places. North Carolina discovered that it had not one or two minority groups but scores, that all of us belonged to one such group or another.

Self-recognition and sometimes strident self-assertion by subgroups appeared to be a new and permanent component of social and cultural relations. From every quarter arose the demand that respect be accorded on equal terms to all groups and, ultimately, to every individual. There might remain ways of circumventing the demand; there seemed to be no prospect of squelching it. To be a Tar Heel was no longer to be white, male, adult, and middle class only; the term now had wider meaning and content, a new promise for all North Carolinians of the spiritual and material benefits of the good life.

Acknowledgments

The efforts of many persons have gone into this work. The suggestions that resulted from our public appeal for information as well as the knowledge of experts in many areas have enhanced the quality of this book and facilitated its production. Volunteers who led us to privately owned sites and out-of-the-way places have added materially to the gathering and scope of the information in this volume. To all these contributors the staff is sincerely grateful. We especially wish to thank Larry Bennett, Alice Cotten, Jerry Cotten, Bob Farrington, Kirk Fuller, Walton Haywood, Jesse R. Lankford, Jr., Jo White Linn, Malvin E. Moore, J. Robert Morrison, Bob Mosher, Allan Paul, Theresa Pennington, Bob Price, Keith Strawn, Maurice Toler, Ray Whitamore, and Charlene Young.

The staffs of various institutions have also aided our research: the Manuscript Department of the William R. Perkins Library and the University Archives, Duke University; the North Carolina Collection and the Southern Historical Collection of the Louis R. Wilson Library, University of North Carolina at Chapel Hill; the University Archives of the D. H. Hill Library, North Carolina State University; and the Archeology and Historic Preservation, Archives and Records, Historic Sites, Iconographic Records, Historical Publications, and Technical Services areas of the Division of Archives and History, North Carolina Department of Cultural Resources. To all of them it is a pleasure to acknowledge our indebtedness and thanks.

Home demonstrator of the Agricultural Extension Service. N.C. State University Archives.

N.C. State Archives. The Carolina Hotel
in Raleigh is no longer standing. Hotels
like this one—the Sir Walter Raleigh
(1923–24) in Raleigh and the Hotel Kinston (1928), Kinston, Lenoir County—
are now refurbished as housing for the
elderly.

Bibliography

Printed Sources

Badger, Anthony J. *Prosperity Road: The New Deal, Tobacco, and North Carolina*. Chapel Hill, 1980.

Barefoot, Pamela, and Kornegay, Burt. *Mules and Memories: A Photo Documentary of the Tobacco Farmer*. Winston-Salem, 1978.

Bledsoe, Jerry. *The World's Number One, Flat-Out, All-Time Great Stock Car Racing Book*. Garden City, N.Y., 1975.

Blythe, LeGette. *William Henry Belk*. Chapel Hill, 1950.

Boyd, William K. *The Story of Durham: City of the New South*. Durham, 1925.

Brinton, Hugh Penn. "The Negro in Durham." Ph.D. dissertation, University of North Carolina at Chapel Hill, 1930.

Burlington Industries, Inc. *The Spencer Love Story*. Burlington, N.C., 1962.

Carter, Wilmoth. *The Urban Negro in the South*. New York, 1961.

Chafe, William H. *Civilities and Civil Rights: Greensboro, North Carolina, and the Black Struggle for Freedom*. New York, 1980.

Clay, James W., and Orr, Douglas M., Jr. *Metrolina Atlas*. Chapel Hill, 1972.

———; Orr, Douglas M., Jr.; and Stuart, Alfred W. *North Carolina Atlas: Portrait of a Changing Southern State*. Chapel Hill, 1975.

Coates, Albert. *By Her Own Bootstraps: A Saga of Women in North Carolina*. Chapel Hill, 1975.

Cope, Robert F., and Wellman, Manly Wade. *The County of Gaston*. Charlotte, 1961.

Cox, William E. *Southern Sidelights*. Raleigh, 1942.

Craig, M. Eleanor. "Recent History of the North Carolina Furniture Manufacturing Industry with Special Attention to Locational Factors." Ph.D. dissertation, Duke University, 1959.

Daniels, Jonathan. "North Carolina." *Holiday*, October 1947.

———. *Tar Heels: A Portrait of North Carolina*. New York, 1941.

Dickey, J. A., and Branson, E. C. *How Farm Tenants Live: A Social-Economic Survey in Chatham County, N.C.* Chapel Hill, 1922.

Federal Writers' Project. *North Carolina: A Guide to the Old North State*. Chapel Hill, 1939.

Gatewood, Willard B., Jr. *Preachers, Pedagogues, and Politics, 1920–1927*. Chapel Hill, 1966.

Ginns, Patsy Moore. *Rough Weather Makes Good Timber: Carolinians Recall*. Chapel Hill, 1977.

Grant, Joanne, ed. *Black Protest History: Documents and Analyses, 1619 to the Present*. New York, 1968.

Harden, John. *North Carolina Roads and Their Builders*. Vol. 2. Raleigh, 1966.

Hagood, Margaret Jarman. *Mothers of the South: Portraiture of the White Tenant Farm Woman*. Chapel Hill, 1939.

Harrill, L. R. *Memories of 4-H*. Raleigh, 1967.

Herring, Harriet L. *Passing of the Mill Village*. Chapel Hill, 1949.

Hobbs, S. Huntington. *North Carolina: An Economic and Social Profile*. Chapel Hill, 1958.

Hodges, Luther H. *Businessman in the State House: Six Years as Governor of North Carolina*. Chapel Hill, 1962.

Howard, Donald S. *The WPA and Federal Relief Policy*. New York, 1943.

Jackson, Annis Ward. "Reflections of a Moonshiner: The Life and Times of Willard Watson." *Tar Heel*, April 1980.

Kaufman, Naomi. "Minister Hoped to Wreck Segregation." *Durham Morning Herald*, 9 December 1979.

Lefler, Hugh T., and Newsome, Albert R. *North Carolina: The History of a Southern State*. 3d ed. Chapel Hill, 1973.

Marcello, Ronald E. "The North Carolina Works Progress Administration and the Politics of Relief." Ph.D. dissertation, Duke University, 1968.

Marteena, Constance H. *The Lengthening Shadow of a Woman: A Biography of Charlotte Hawkins Brown*. Hicksville, N.Y., 1977.

McKimmon, Jane S. *When We're Green We Grow*. Chapel Hill, 1945.

Moore, James L., and Wingate, Thomas H. *Cabarrus Reborn: A Historical Sketch of the Founding and Development of Cannon Mills Company and Kannapolis*. Kannapolis, N.C., 1940.

Murray, Pauli. *Proud Shoes: The Story of an American Family*. New York, 1956.

Myers, James. *Field Notes: Textile Strikes in South*. New York, 1929.

Parramore, Thomas C. *Carolina Quest*. Englewood Cliffs, N.J., 1978.

Paths Toward Freedom: A Biographical History of Blacks and Indians in North Carolina by Blacks and Indians. Raleigh, 1976.

Pierce, Walter H. *Trends in the Development of Agriculture in North Carolina*. Raleigh, 1965.

Powell, William S., ed. *Dictionary of North Carolina Biography*, Vol. 1. Chapel Hill, 1979.

Powledge, Fred. "Going Home to Raleigh." *Harper's Magazine*, April 1970.

Read, Martha Norburn. *Asheville . . . in the Land of the Sky*. Richmond, 1942.

Robinson, Blackwell P., ed. *The North Carolina Guide*. Chapel Hill, 1955.

Rutledge, William E., Jr. *An Illustrated History of Yadkin County, 1850–1965*. Yadkinville, N.C., 1965.

Salmond, John A. *The Civilian Conservation Corps, 1933–1942*. Durham, 1967.

Saunders, W. O. *The Book of Ham*. Elizabeth City, N.C., 1924.

Sewell, Joseph L. "The Only Negro Deaf-Mute Lawyer in the United States." *The Silent Worker*, March 1927.

Shackelford, Laurel, and Weinberg, Bill. *Our Appalachia: An Oral History*. New York, 1977.

Sharpe, Bill. *Tar on My Heels*. Winston-Salem, 1946.

Taylor, Rosser H. *Carolina Crossroads*. Murfreesboro, N.C., 1966.

Terrill, Tom E., and Hirsch, Jerrold. *Such as Us: Southern Voices of the Thirties*. Chapel Hill, 1978.

Terkel, Studs. *Hard Times: An Oral History of the Great Depression*. New York, 1970.

U.S. Army Corps of Engineers, Board of Engineers for Rivers and Harbors. *The Port of Wilmington, N.C.* Pt. 2. Washington, D.C., 1961.

Watson, Helen R. "The Grocery Stores of Yesteryear." *The State*, March 1980.

Waynick, Capus. *North Carolina Roads and Their Builders*. Vol. 1. Raleigh, 1952.

Weare, Walter B. *Black Business in the New South: A Social History of the North Carolina Mutual Life Insurance Company*. Urbana, Ill., 1973.

Wilson: A Special Supplement to the New East Magazine. Greenville, N.C., 1973.

Wilson, Terry P. *The Cart that Changed the World*. Norman, Okla., 1978.

Wolcott, Reed M. *Rose Hill*. New York, 1976.

Wolfe, Tom. "The Last American Hero is Junior Johnson, *Yes!*" *Esquire*, March 1965.

Wolfe, Thomas. *Look Homeward, Angel*. New York, 1929.

Newspapers and Magazines

Greensboro Daily News (special edition), 29 May 1971.

Research and Farming.

The State.

Tar Heel: The Magazine of North Carolina.

We the People of North Carolina.

Clipping File, North Carolina Collection, Louis R. Wilson Library, University of North Carolina, Chapel Hill.

Manuscript Sources

Manuscript Department, William R. Perkins Library, Duke University, Durham.

Durham Chamber of Commerce Papers.

Robert P. Harriss Papers.

Hemphill Family Papers.

North Carolina Collection, Louis R. Wilson Library, University of North Carolina, Chapel Hill.

Stutz, Carleton, and Maxfield, Peter A. "Tobacco Bag Stringing Operations in North Carolina and Virginia." Richmond, 1939.

Southern Historical Collection, Louis R. Wilson Library, University of North Carolina, Chapel Hill.

Howard W. Odum Subregional Photo Study.

Southern Oral History Program (SOHP), University of North Carolina, Chapel Hill.

Julius Fry, interviewed by William Finger.

Zelma Murray, interviewed by Brent Glass.

Lacy Wright, interviewed by William Finger and Charles Hughes.

1 Graham County

Fontana Dam and Village.
Joyce Kilmer Memorial Forest, *Nantahala National Forest*

Haywood County

I-40 between Cove Creek and Tenn. line.

Henderson County

Curb Market, *Hendersonville*.

Buncombe County

Asheville High School.
Battery Park Hotel, *Asheville*.
Biltmore House, *Asheville*.
City Hall, Pack Square, *Asheville*.
First Baptist Church, *Asheville*.
Grove Park Inn, *Asheville*.
The New Arcade, Federal Building, *Asheville*.
Thomas Wolfe Memorial, *Asheville*.

Yancey County

Carolina Hemlock Park, *south of Celo*.

Alleghany County to Swain County

Blue Ridge Parkway.

Gaston County

Cramerton Mills, *Cramerton*.
Loray Mill, *Gastonia*.

2 Mecklenburg County

William Henry Belk Hall, Davidson College, *Davidson*.
Latta Arcade, *Charlotte*.
Mint Museum of Art, *Charlotte*.

Cabarrus County

Charlotte Motor Speedway, *Harrisburg*.

Yadkin County

Yadkin Basket Company, *Yadkinville*.

Rowan County

Pope and Airy Store, *Salisbury*.

Stanly County

Morrow Mountain State Park.

Forsyth County

North Carolina School of the Arts, *Winston-Salem*.

Rockingham County

Warf's Airport, *Reidsville*.

Guilford County

Carolina Theatre, *Greensboro*.
High Point Museum.
Irvin Arcade, *Greensboro*.
Jefferson Standard Building, *Greensboro*.
Kress Building, *Greensboro*.
Southern Furniture Exposition Building, *High Point*.
Thomas Built Buses, Inc., *High Point*.
Woolworth's, *Greensboro*.

Moore County

Bellview Schoolhouse, Board of Education grounds, *U.S. #1 south of Sanford*.
Weymouth Woods Sandhills Nature Preserve, *Southern Pines*.

Orange County

Brady's Restaurant, *Chapel Hill*.
Pleasant Green Church, *Pleasant Green Rd., near Cole Mill Rd*.
Schley Grange.

Map of Historic Places

3 Durham County
Burroughs Wellcome Company, *Research Triangle Park*.
Carolina Theatre, *Durham*.
Duke Chapel, Duke University, *Durham*.
Duke Homestead, *Durham*.
IBM Corporation, *Research Triangle Park*.
Mechanics and Farmers Bank, *Durham*.
Monsanto Triangle Park Development Center, *Research Triangle Park*.
North Carolina Mutual Life Insurance Company, *Durham*.
Patterson's Mill Country Store, *Farrington Road*.

Wake County
Cameron Village, *Raleigh*.
Memorial Auditorium, *Raleigh*.
North Carolina Museum of History, *Raleigh*.
North Carolina Museum of Art, *Raleigh*.

Warren County
Chapel of the Good Shepherd, *Ridgeway vicinity*.
Roses Store, *Warrenton*.

Bladen County
Singletary Lake.

Wayne County
Mount Olive Pickle Company.

Wilson County
Smith's Warehouse, *Wilson*.

Halifax County
Roses Store, *Littleton*.

Lenoir County
DuPont Dacron Plant, *N.C. #11 east of Kinston*.

Pitt County
Shiloh Church, *Penny Hill vicinity*.

4 New Hanover County
Castle Hayne.
North Carolina Ports Authority, *Wilmington*.
Wilmington Memorial Bridge.

Pender County
Penderlea.
St. Helena.

Carteret County
Cedar Island Ferry.

Craven County
Tryon Palace, *New Bern*.

Beaufort County
Terra Ceia.

Hyde County
Lake Mattamuskeet National Wildlife Refuge.
Ocracoke Ferry.
Swan Quarter National Wildlife Refuge.

Tyrrell County
Lindsay C. Warren Bridge, *U.S. #64*.

Dare County
Herbert Bonner Bridge, *N.C. #12*.
Fort Raleigh National Historic Site, *Roanoke Island*.
Hatteras Ferry.

Currituck County
Currituck Ferry.

Index